SIMPLE

JAPANESE

FURNITURE

SIMPLE
JAPANESE
FURNITURE

24 MID-CENTURY PROJECTS FOR YOUR HOME

group monomono

THE GUILD OF MASTER CRAFTSMAN PUBLICATIONS

CONTENTS

01 CHAIRS

02 TABLES

03 STORAGE

INTRODUCTION

This book is based on *Aidia wo ikashita katei no kosaku* or *Making Use of Ingenious Ideas: Woodworking at Home*, first published in 1953 by the handicraft publishing company Ondori-sha and put together by the industrial design group KAK. This new edition, compiled by Group monomono, breathes new life into the original mid-century designs and shows off their enduring appeal for modern homes.

In the 1950s, there wasn't much ready-made household furniture available. Shelves, desks and other household furniture items were built at home. Carpentry wasn't just a hobby in those times, it was an essential skill in life. In this updated and revised form, you will find simple and functional household items that will have a place in homes today, with an appealing mid-century style that still looks fresh. Focusing on wooden furniture, it introduces 24 stylish furniture pieces along with detailed step-by-step photographs, drawings and instructions.

A note on materials
This book only focuses on wooden furniture, even though the original publication included other materials, such as plastic. Many of the projects in this book were created using Japanese cedar (*Cryptomeria japonica*), a conscious choice to promote this versatile and widely available material to the Japanese readership. It may not be possible to easily source Japanese cedar in other parts of the world but there are alternatives that work equally well for these projects, such as Larch and Tulipwood. If you can't find these, look for various other softwoods that are available in your area, make sure they have a fairly tight grain and are as knot-free as possible.

USING THIS BOOK

Title of
each piece

Difficulty
level and time
required for
making

Explanation
of key points
found in each
project

How each work
was originally
published

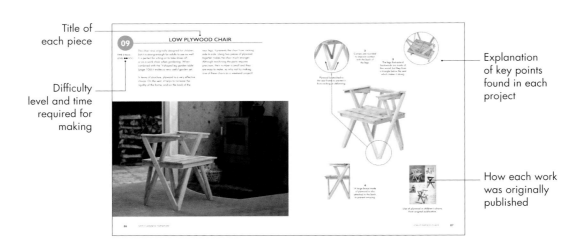

Parts and
materials
needed

Tools used

Indicates
dimensions of
the parts to be
cut from the
material

Finished
drawings
showing
placement
of the parts

The unit of
measurements
used throughout
is millimetres.
There is a
detailed metric
to imperial
conversion
chart on
page 182

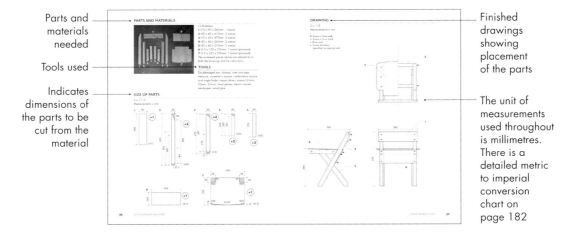

EXPLORING THE ORIGINAL BOOK

In 1953, the industrial design group KAK was formed in Meguro, Tokyo. The three young members of KAK, Yoshio Akioka, Junnosuke Kawa and Itaru Kaneko, dreamed of new forms of post-war industrial design. Their optical instruments, like the Sekonic Colour Meter and Minolta Camera, went on to have huge success, but their first project was to produce the book entitled, *Making Use of Ingenious Ideas: Woodworking at Home.*

FUNCTION AND DESIGN

The book reflected the personality of the individual KAK members — each of whom believed in the benefits of manual work and relished the pursuit of true pleasure found in such labour. The KAK's first project aimed to create various items that project images of a joyful home using minimal high-quality tools.

As the title implies, *Woodworking at Home* was filled with desirable items for any household and just setting eyes upon them would thrill anyone. Chairs, tables, an umbrella stand, bookshelves, pen stands, dog houses, toy boxes, etc. These items were all presented with many photographs and interesting commentaries. Along with a variety of construction tips, the items were presented in such a manner as to consider both how the item would be seen when it was placed in a room and what sort of image the item would create in that space. The book treated the functionality of each item as part of its design.

The beginning of the book provided instructions for acquiring tools. You may think that purchasing the most economical tools would be sufficient for home woodworking tasks. However, as the book suggested, it is best to buy professional-grade tools because, once purchased, they would last for decades. There was also a guide to saws, chisels, awls, nails, whetstones and other tools, including hand planes, the most difficult tool to use for non-professionals.

UNIQUE DRAWINGS

The last half of the book presented drawings of each item. The layout of those pages was graphically pleasing due to the combination of black line drawings on a yellow background.

A love of tools and woodworking, plus a desire to not overthink things and simply take action were commonly shared feelings among the members of KAK. The energy generated by the union of these ideas led to *Woodworking at Home.* This book was different from other DIY books of the time because it wasn't just about making furniture, it also took into consideration a family's everyday life. It incorporated styles that genuinely helped the reader to spend everyday life as pleasantly and comfortably as possible.

Making Use of Ingenious Ideas: Woodworking at Home, published by Ondori-sha, 1953.

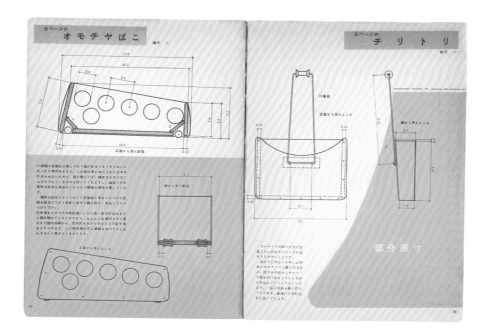

The distinctive style of black drawings over a yellow background.

Left: 'Cute and easy-to-make plywood toy box'. Right: 'Easy-to-use dustpan made of celluloid underlay and plywood'.

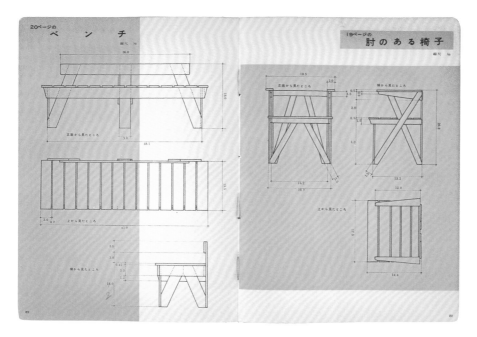

Left: 'Bench in a bright garden'. Right: 'Sturdy comfortable chair with armrest'.

'This book was different from other DIY books of the time because it wasn't just about making furniture, it also took into consideration a family's everyday life.'

'Easy-to-use dustpan made of celluloid underlay and plywood'.

'A tray for safely carrying beer'.

SIMPLE EVERYDAY ITEMS

Among the items presented were, 'A tray for safely carrying a beer bottle' and 'A dustpan that helps to neatly sweep the corners of a room' (see above). The names were quite unique and often comical. The authors at KAK observed their everyday lives and then created items they felt would be useful. They made sure to use effective, simplified designs. They also created 'A cart for carrying a rice cooking pot'. This reflected the social conditions of the time as it was before electric rice-cookers were found in almost every Japanese household (Toshiba introduced the first electric rice-cooker in 1955).

One of the most practical and unique items was a hanging lamp that made use of a curtain rod. The lamp was attached to the narrow metal railing installed on a wall. The lamp shade hung upside-down (thus, appearing as an inverse trapezoid). The lamp slid on the rod, so you could move it wherever you wanted. Items created from such brilliant ideas provide timeless inspiration that would lead almost anyone to attempt to create them. The book also introduced another very convenient lamp that could be a wall hanging or a simple table lamp. This particular lamp is still being used to this day at one of Akioka's relative's home.

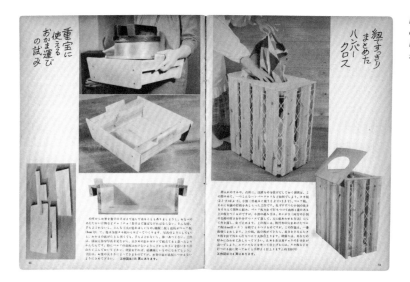

Left: 'A rice cooking pot cart'. Right: 'Neat storage hamper'.

Left: 'A hanging lamp that slides on a curtain rod'. Right: 'Curtain fittings can be used to make beautiful bamboo curtains'.

Mitsubishi Uni pencils.

INNOVATIVE MATERIALS

Finally, *Woodworking at Home* inventively selected and provided material commentaries. The book primarily used pieces of wood planking and plywood because they were so widely available. In addition, KAK had chosen to use celluloid sheeting as a relatively inexpensive alternative. The use of celluloid sheets is a typical KAK-like idea, which often accentuates the space in a house. The items in, 'A fun letter holder and bookends made of celluloid sheeting' and 'A novel mail box that effectively uses celluloid sheeting', were manufactured by warming celluloid sheets and then moulding them. This use of celluloid material can be said to be a precursor to the packaging for the Mitsubishi Uni pencils (1958), which KAK would later undertake (above right). The package design used plastic, not in popular use at the time, and a transparent lid that was secured with aluminium hinges to a box, on which a bold gothic font 'Uni' was printed. The unusual design was thought to be revolutionary. Akioka's talent was conceiving of such brilliant ideas. From the original, *Woodworking at Home*, it is not hard to imagine the faces of KAK members – Akioka, Kawa and Kaneko – joyously coming up with such creations.

Furihata Chikako
(Curator, Meguro Museum of Art)

WHY LOOK BACK NOW?

I first encountered KAK's *Woodworking at Home* in 2011 at the 'DOMA Yoshio Akioka Exhibition' held at the Meguro Museum of Art. At the exhibition, which included not only his accomplishments as an industrial designer but also Akioka's achievements in other fields such as toys and folk art, I was drawn in by the timeless appeal of this book, even though it was not his most prominent.

THOUGHTFUL DESIGN

The exhibition contained a collection of simple instructions and drawings that woodworking amateurs could use to produce an entire range of chairs, tables and storage units. In other words, the book was a DIY guidebook. However, it wasn't just a manual. It was a collection of products that responded to the demand for works that targeted the field of 'novice DIY'. The items presented were thoughtfully designed for ease of construction.

Using materials and tools that are readily available allows DIY amateurs to construct items economically and simply just as much now as it did when the book was first published. In fact, many of the materials used in *Woodworking at Home* are generally considered to be unsuitable for making furniture. For example, the rough-cut cedar boards. It would be easy to write this off as an excuse for low quality or bad design. But, for the KAK members, 'readily available materials' and the 'skill level of amateurs' were just the given conditions that determined their designs. They always considered the properties of the materials, how to combine them, cost and the dimensions of the components before integrating everything in a brilliant way.

What KAK achieved was the work of very high-level designers. They always had a thorough understanding of material characteristics and determined feasible structures based on the tools and woodworking skills of the target audience. They delivered designs while considering assembly methods and taking into consideration distribution of structural forces. Their goals have always been far from the trivial idea of 'making cool shapes'. Once Yoshio Akioka said, 'Cherish items you have, don't be a consumer (of mass-produced goods).' That's why I think that what *Woodworking at Home* presented wasn't just 'things' rather it was 'life' brought about by utilizing the items presented.

AN ITALIAN CONNECTION

A similar book entitled *Autoprogettazione?*, published in 1974, was written by Italian designer Enzo Mari, 21 years after KAK's *Woodworking at Home*. This book also presents photos and drawings of easily constructed furniture using inexpensive, readily available materials. Enzo Mari was a designer who created products for high-end furniture manufacturers such as DANESE and DRIADE, and on the surface he seemed to be very far away from the DIY world (just like KAK who designed cameras and motorcycles). What drew both to DIY, even though they came from different times and countries?

When *Autoprogettazione?* was published, Italy was facing an economic crisis, meaning social conditions weren't favourable to selling high-end products. By contrast, Japan was in the midst of post-war reconstruction and rapid economic growth, fuelled by the special economic demands of the Korean War in 1953. Economic despair and economic hope, polar opposites experienced by Enzo and KAK. What both have in common is an awareness that under extreme economic conditions, economic logic runs out of control, thus stripping 'life' from the relationship between goods and society, and subsequently alienating people.

Both KAK and Enzo Mari sought something beyond designing mere goods. Rather, they attempted to capture, through their products, qualities of real life, as well as the time that

Left: Akioka and KAK staff member Kazuo Shibata (right) sit on a bench in the courtyard of Akioka's house where the KAK office is located in Meguro Ward, Tokyo.

Below: Meguro Museum of Art Spring 2017 exhibition. In the foreground, furniture from Woodworking at Home, made by Satoru Ito, is displayed.

flows through it. I think their DIY designs were a result of attempts to find a way to get people involved, especially when they sensed disruption between their work and people's lives.

I would like to introduce a passage from Yoshio Akioka's book, From Chopsticks to Cars (1971). 'Make things with your hands that are necessary in everyday life. I believe this is the original idea behind manufacturing... Let's take a look at modern manufacturing. In today's specialized production systems, the designer, the maker, the seller and the buyer are all completely different people. In such a system, you are just a person who consumes something that someone else thought of, or something that somebody else made. I am a designer, a person who thinks. My designs materialize through the work of others and are sold by others.'

Akioka was concerned about differentiation brought about by the division of labour, and found his role as a designer as breaking through that division. He considered how to negotiate relationships between various entities in the production system and users. We certainly get a glimpse of this spirit in Woodworking at Home.

Satoru Ito
(Architect, Assistant Professor at Toyo University)

ABOUT THE KAK DESIGN GROUP

Formed by three unique designers in September 1953, the same year that NHK television started broadcasting, Japan's first corporate industrial design firm, KAK Design Group, was established by Yoshio Akioka, Junnosuke Kawa and Itaru Kaneko. Named according to the initials of the three founding members, it was an interesting collaboration that has created many unique masterpieces ranging from radio cabinets, cameras, and optical equipment to motorcycles and even paper products. KAK has taken up a unique position in Japanese industrial design.

'There is meaning in forming a team where people with different values and specialties can come together.'

Junnosuke Kawa, Yoshio Akioka and Itaru Kaneko.
This photo was taken by a member of the staff, but
they also liked to take portraits of each other. A large
number of them have been preserved.

SAW WITH BACKBONE (AZEBIKI TIP)

A single-edged saw, reinforced with a metal backbone. The body is thin and the blade fine, resulting in a clean cut. Used when you need to cut carefully along a line, such as cutting notches.

Azebiki tip
The blade tip is in the shape of an arc. It can be used to make incision cuts because it can start cutting mid-panel. (It is used on page 60.)

KEYHOLE SAW

A saw for cutting curved lines. The blade is thin to fit around curves. Used only when perpendicular to the material. See page 174.

HAMMER

Mainly used for hammering in nails and striking chisels. It is best to choose a hammer that is not too heavy.

CHISEL

Can be used to drill holes and chamfer parts by tapping with a hammer. Mainly used for chipping here. Three blade widths, 9mm, 15mm and 24mm are sufficient.

HAND PLANE

Used to shave surfaces thinly to flatten. The amount of protruding blade should be just a hair's breadth. For beginners, we recommend planes where the blade can be easily replaced once dull.

SQUARE

The short side is called the tongue and the long side is called the body. The tongue can be thicker and hooked onto the material to accurately draw perpendicular lines. Also used to check for right angles at key points.

ANGLE FINDER

The angle can be adjusted by loosening the screw. This is very useful for capturing drawing angles and marking the material. This is one of the essential items in this manual.

RULER

Also called a straightedge, 150mm or 300mm is sufficient.

CARPENTER'S SQUARE

Tool used to measure length and to find right angles. Unlike regular squares, the thickness is uniform. It can also be used to draw longer perpendicular lines down the middle of the material.

TAPE MEASURE

Used to measure long distances. A wide tape measure that will not distort or twist is recommended. A length of at least 2m is required.

CLAMP

Used to fix materials or jigs to a workbench. Also used for various other purposes, such as temporarily fastening materials together. It is best to have several clamps available at any given time.

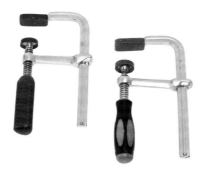

SANDPAPER

Used to smooth surfaces or remove small amounts of material. Wrap around your hand or a piece of wood. Medium to fine grit (200–400) is recommended.

IMPACT DRIVER

Can be used for both driving and drilling. It has a very desirable torque adjustment function to prevent over-tightening or jamming of screws.

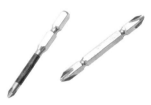

Phillips head bit
Bits for driving screws. There are various sizes, but for the purpose of this manual, sizes +1 and +2 are sufficient.

Countersink bit
A bit with a shoulder at the base for countersinking pre-drilled holes. Can be shaped to fit the head of your countersink screws.

Pre-drilling bit
A long, thin bit for pre-drilling holes. The thickness of the bit should be thinner than the neck of the screw you will be using. This will help prevent stripping.

Auger bit
A bit with a cutter for drilling larger holes. Available in various diameters. Used in this book on page 122.

Right-angle bit
Used to drill screws in tight spaces where the drill body cannot fit. Used on page 67 of this manual.

ELECTRIC SANDER

Sandpaper can be easily replaced because the pad uses hook and loop tape. Very efficient when sanding large areas.

BRASS NAILS

A rust-resistant, attractive nail used to attach tabletops and seats. Helical nails have greater holding power but require more force to drive.

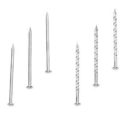

SCREWS

Used to fasten two pieces of wood together. It is recommended that the length of the screw be at least twice the thickness of the material to be fastened.

CORRUGATED NAILS

Wave-shaped nails used to align and join two boards on their ends. They are hammered into the ends of your pieces.

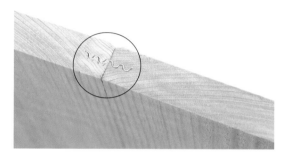

Angle-cut cross section

WOOD GLUE

Adhesive used to join wood. Can be used to reinforce screws and to increase strength by applying it to joint surfaces.

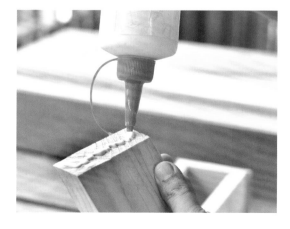

BOX CUTTER

Use a box cutter instead of a pencil when you want to draw super fine lines. Using a box cutter to draw your chisel's working line will prevent the material from sinking in as you chisel. This allows for a much cleaner finish.

FINISHES

Paint is used to improve not just the design of the work, by adding lustre or changing colour, but also to prevent staining, water damage and weathering. While unpainted wood allows you to enjoy the natural texture and ageing of the wood, painting can make it last longer, so be sure to choose a paint that suits your purpose and produces a fine finish.

POLYURETHANE PAINT
Paint that produces a strong film and also improves waterproofing properties. Water and stain resistant.

WOOD STAIN
Used to impregnate wood and colour it to bring out the grain. Weather resistant and preservative.

OUTDOOR PAINT
Has weather resistance and preservative properties. Ideal for furniture used outdoors.

OPAQUE PAINT
Creates a coloured film of paint.

NATURAL FINISHES
These include substances such as persimmon tannin, and oil finishes such as linseed oil and perilla oil. They are safe even if you ingest them by mistake. Stain resistant and preservative.

SOURCING WOOD

All the furniture in this book is made from building materials sold at DIY stores and timber suppliers. One of the most used materials is cedar planking (see page 7 for a list of alternative types of wood). The thickness and width are standardized. Once you have decided on the furniture you want to make, calculate how many different types of boards you will need and how many pieces (lengths) you will need in total. Some of the longest boards are more than 2m long, so it is a good idea to have them cut to length at the store, making them easier to carry and process.

First, work out what standard measurements and lengths of material are available at your local store. Wooden planks tend to warp and twist so choose materials that are as straight and clean as possible.

Your timber supplier should have a cutting service where they will cut with a machine for a fee. If you prepare a drawing with all the cutting dimensions written down in advance, ordering will go smoothly.

TOOL TECHNIQUES

USING SAWS

BASIC SAW GRIPS

The most important thing to remember when sawing is to hold the material firmly in place and use your entire arm to saw. Once you learn to saw in a straight line, you will be able to quickly, and accurately, cut material.

1 Check that the saw is vertical and following the marked line, by examining from directly above.

2 Line up the nose and saw blade directly above the marked line.

3 Lean over slightly. Allow your arm to move straight back.

4 The best height for a workbench is one where you can move your elbows comfortably.

5 Move your entire arm. Keep shoulder, elbow and hand in line so that you can saw at a consistent angle.

6 Relax your grip as much as possible. Hold primarily with your little finger and support with your other fingers.

7 Secure the material with clamps, or other means, as necessary.

TIPS FOR CUTTING

Use your left thumb to align the blade with the marked line. Be sure to take the thickness of the saw blade into account. Hold at a shallow angle and lightly push the blade along the marked line several times to make a 'path'.

The saw cuts more when pulled towards you. Hold at an angle of about 30 degrees and use the entire length of the blade. If sawing becomes too difficult, increase or decrease the angle and then continue.

TIPS FOR NOTCHING

Start a shallow cut at the front of the material and gradually raise the saw. Continue until the saw is perpendicular to the marked line. Keep a close eye on both the front and back of the material so as not to cross the black line.

HOW TO MARK OUT LINES

One of the most important parts of the process is properly marking out your lines. This involves reading the dimensions from the drawing and transferring them to the material correctly.

Two tools that are very useful for this process are the square and the angle finder. Always use them to increase accuracy and efficiency.

USING A SQUARE

Tongue

Body

1 Place tongue end on material. Be careful not to accidentally angle the tongue end.

2 Use a pencil (or box cutter) to mark endpoints. Use a straight edge or ruler to mark off the length between points.

3 Rotate the material 90 degrees. Align the square along the material. Line up the end of the black line marked in step 2 with the body of the square. Now you have black lines on two sides.

4 Turn and mark the last two sides. This way, the progress of the cut can be checked from each of the four sides.

USING AN ANGLE FINDER

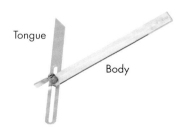

Tongue

Body

1 Loosen the centre screw and place the angle finder on the drawing. It may be useful to enlarge the drawing using a photocopier. Align the tongue with the desired line, set the angle and tighten the screw.

2 Align the body along the material and mark the angle with a pencil (or cutter).

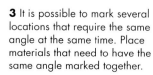

3 It is possible to mark several locations that require the same angle at the same time. Place materials that need to have the same angle marked together.

USING AN IMPACT DRIVER

BASIC STANCE FOR AN IMPACT DRIVER

The most important thing to remember when handling an impact driver is to apply weight (force) to the drill bit on its central axis. If you learn how to apply force correctly, you can use a driver in a variety of positions. This handy tool allows you to both tighten screws and drill holes easily, so be sure to master it.

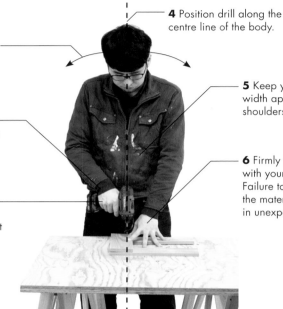

1 The upper body should be poised so that the tip of the bit can be seen.

2 Tighten your arms, centred around your navel, so that you can apply more force.

3 Tighten the little finger and loosely support it with other fingers. This will lock your wrist and arm in place and make it easier to apply force.

4 Position drill along the centre line of the body.

5 Keep your feet shoulder-width apart and relax your shoulders.

6 Firmly fix the material with your hand or clamps. Failure to do so may cause the material to rotate, resulting in unexpected injury.

DRIVING SCREWS IN STRAIGHT

Set the screw and move the head back and forth to make sure the tip is pointing straight down in the direction you wish to drill. Use the same method when drilling holes.

To prevent the bit from skidding off the screw head, stiffen your wrist and apply force only along the screw direction.

USEFUL TERMS

ANGLE BRACE
Structural piece that supports a horizontally extending member diagonally from below.

BACK PLATE
A piece of wood placed on material to prevent damage when hammering.

BRACE
A member that connects the legs of a piece of furniture horizontally.

BURR
When cutting materials with a saw or similar tool, this is the wispy material left behind.

CHAMFER
To finish off corners by removing angles with a hand plane or sandpaper.

CROSS BRACING
Material that is crossed and attached on the diagonal between posts, legs, etc.

CROSS-CUT
To saw across the fibres of the wood.

DRY FIT
Assembling without glue and checking whether the joints and positioning of the parts are correct.

END GRAIN
The cross-section of a piece of wood when it is cut at right angles to the fibre direction.

FLUSH
A flush surface simply means there is no unevenness between parts butted together.

FRAME
A set of parts that connect together to support the structure.

HALF JOINT
Joint where two pieces of material are interlocked by chipping out notches.

INTERNAL ANGLE
The inner part of a corner formed when two planes intersect at an angle.

JIG
General term for auxiliary tools and devices to perform a given task more efficiently.

MARKING
To make marks on the material to be processed. It is best to use a thin pencil for accuracy.

PLYWOOD
Board made by laminating an odd number of thinly sliced veneers along grain direction.

PRE-DRILLED HOLES
A small hole drilled in advance to ensure that screws or nails are driven in at the correct position and angle.

RIGIDITY
Property of a structure (or material) that resists bending or twisting.

RIP CUT
To saw parallel to wood fibre direction.

SIDE PLATE/SIDE PANEL
A board placed on the side of a piece of furniture when viewed from the front.

SKIRTING
A rectangular piece of wood, in the shape of a rail, attached to the underside of a drawer

TRANSPOSE
To copy dimensions or angles from a drawing or other source.

WRAPAROUND MARKING
Type of marking whereby a line is drawn on one side of a square piece of wood, and then the line is extended to all four sides.

STRUCTURAL DESCRIPTIONS

The style of furniture in this book includes unique ideas for sturdy construction using cedar boards and plywood. This page provides examples and explanations of how things work.

V-SHAPED LEGS

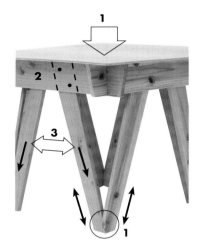

The V-shaped leg structure is made by joining the ends of two legs that extend downwards diagonally from adjacent positions. Splitting the base of the legs in two allows the structure to efficiently distribute force and adds strength. This structure is effective when using thin materials. Can also be called a truss.

1 Loads applied to the top surface are spread across two members and down to one leg tip, and that leg tip tightens. Conversely, load applied to each leg tip is dispersed in two directions to distribute force.

2 Works best when all components are firmly fixed to the frame.

3 The angles of the legs make this piece resistant to racking, or swaying back and forth.

> **Note on resizing**
> By changing the length of the two frame pieces facing each other, without changing the size of the V-shaped legs, it is possible to manufacture this product in any size. If the length of the framing pieces exceeds 450mm, add a brace in the middle to support the top (seat) so it doesn't sag.

CROSS BRACING/ANGLE BRACING

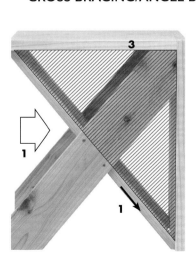
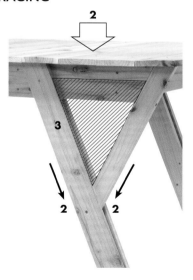

Cross bracing is a diagonally intersecting member that prevents deformation. Angle braces are structural supports that extend up from below at an angle, efficiently transferring load to the legs.

1 Cross bracing stands up to horizontal forces and distributes them.

2 Angle bracing takes top surface load and efficiently transfers it to the leg tips.

3 Both types of bracing help maintain the distance between the horizontally and vertically extended members and prevent them from deforming.

SCISSOR-LEG CONSTRUCTION

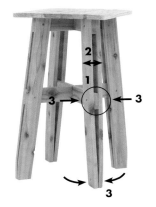

This is a structure in which the frame and/or bracing is sandwiched between two boards, which are then screwed together. It is easy to make, with the same strength as a tenon, but without the difficulty of making an actual tenon. Squeezing the leg ends 'clamps' the members together firmly and stabilizes the structure. This is a unique structure that works even when employing thin pieces of wood for the legs.

1 Sandwiching makes it possible to create items with the same strength as a mortise and tenon structure.

2 The legs will, in effect, have the same thickness as three pieces of wood, which will increase the strength and stability of the legs.

3 By squeezing the leg ends, pressure is applied to the pinched member, increasing its holding power.

REINFORCEMENT

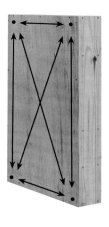

When thin or slender materials are assembled in an 'R' shape, they tend to deform diagonally due to lateral forces. Attaching plywood minimizes deformation. Such structures can be easily reinforced to make them stable.

NOTCHED STRUCTURE

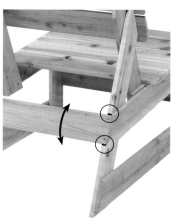

For this structure only one of the components is notched. Cutting out a notch that is the thickness of the brace, and then fixing the members together, makes the structure much stronger than if pieces were fastened with screws in the normal fashion.

CHAIRS

Chairs, which require both comfort and safety, can be difficult to make. This is why one feels such great satisfaction once these projects are complete. Ten unique works are presented in this chapter – from easy-to-construct stools for beginners, to benches and armchairs targeted at intermediate and advanced woodworkers.

01 **Two-way cross-braced stool,**
page 32

02 **Stool with pinched legs,**
page 38

03 **Chair with V-shaped legs,**
page 44

04 **Triangular garden chair,**
page 50

05 **Box-shaped bench,**
page 56

(06) **Pinched-leg high chair,**
page 62

(07) **V-shaped leg garden bench,**
page 68

(08) **Sturdy porch bench,**
page 74

(09) **V-shaped leg armchair,**
page 80

(10) **Low plywood chair,**
page 86

31

TWO-WAY CROSS-BRACED STOOL

You can easily change the seat height of this stool by changing its orientation. Standing the stool upright creates the perfect height for an adult, while tipping it on its side makes the stool the perfect height for a child. This item is also not just a stool, it has a variety of uses. If you put it beside a sofa it becomes a side-table. This stool is not designed to be stood on.

The design element that stands out most is the cross member on the side. It works as a side brace to provide strength against rolling. Also, there is no sense of incongruity whether the stool is upright or on its side. It demonstrates the design philosophy of KAK very well. There are few parts and it is quite easy to construct, so this stool is recommended for beginners.

1

The cross-bracing board attaches at the middle of the 'L' so it provides support against any forces applied to the left, right, top and bottom of the seat.

2

The seat plate is 21mm thick. Such wide and thick boards are very rigid, so just forming an 'L' shape with them will create a strong structure.

3

The corner of the seat plate is heavily chamfered. This makes it comfortable to sit on and, at the same time, has the added benefit of not scarring the floor when the stool is placed on its side.

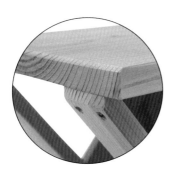

Dual-height stool, from original publication.

PARTS AND MATERIALS

t = thickness
1 t21 x 240 x 310mm: 1 board
2 t21 x 240 x 405mm: 1 board
3 t13 x 90 x 520mm: 2 boards
4 t15 x 45 x 520mm: 2 boards
The numbered pieces above are referred to
in both the drawings and the instructions.

TOOLS

Double-edged saw, clamps, ruler and tape
measure, carpenter's square, combination square
and angle finder, impact driver, screws (50mm,
35mm, 25mm), hand plane, electric sander,
sandpaper, wood glue

SIZE OF PARTS

Scale = 1/10
Measurements = mm

1 240 / 5 / 405 / 5 / (t21) ×1

2 240 / 310 / 5 / (t21) ×1

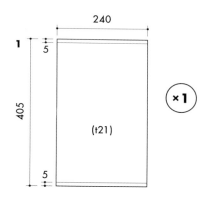

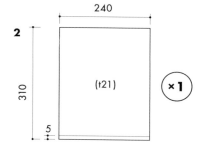

3 90 / 78.5 / 520 / 392 / (t13) / 64.5 ×2

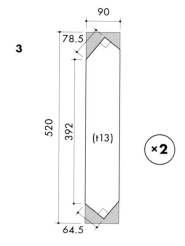

4 45 / 15 / 520 / 475 / 11.5 / Scale = 1/2 / 14.5 / Scale = 1/2 / (t15) ×2

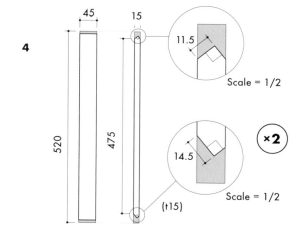

DRAWING

Scale = 1/5
Measurements = mm

- ● Screw in from side
- ● Screw in from back
- ○ Brass nail
- ▶ Screw direction
  (specified as appropriate)

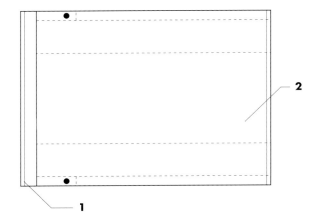

2

1

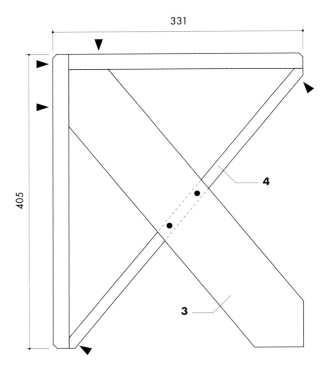

331

405

4

3

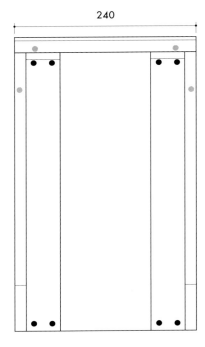

240

1 Use a combination square and angle finder to measure and pencil in the markings. Then cut all the parts using a saw.

2 When creating angles in the parts, cutting from the top is easier and cleaner.

3 Processing thin pieces (**4**) requires a delicate touch. Clamp the part to a workbench. Stabilize the saw blade with your thumb and, using slight pressure, slowly saw through.

4 After processing the material, sand all the parts and chamfer them with a hand plane. Sharp corners can chip easily when first applying the hand plane, so sand them first.

5 To assemble the thick pieces of the L-shaped seat plate (**1, 2**), hold the parts firmly in place when inserting the screw so that the two pieces are even. Inserting the screws is easier if a pilot hole is drilled first. (Screws: 50mm)

6 Place the cross braces (**3, 4**) inside the L-shaped seat plate and screw them together. Make sure both of the braces are symmetrical. (Screws: 35mm)

7 Put the narrower brace part (**4**) inside the angle of the seat plate and insert one screw in each end. Make sure everything is square and check the angle before screwing. (Screws: 25mm)

8 The wide sides of the braces (**3**) should be aligned with the seat plate, as shown. (Screws: 25mm)

9 Screw the wider brace from the outside of the seat plate. The bracing is thin here so drill a pilot hole first, from the outside. This will help keep the screw aligned. (Screws: 50mm)

10 Heavily chamfer the part of the seat plate that comes into contact with the floor and the corner of the L-shape, using a hand plane.

11 When planing off the corners, make sure to shave diagonally. Doing this will prevent the wood from catching in the plane and breaking off the corner.

12 Set the stool on a level surface and check for any wobbling. Adjust the feet with sandpaper or a saw to correct.

STOOL WITH PINCHED LEGS

TIME 3 hours

LEVEL ●●○○○

Weighing just 1.2kg, this is a convenient stool that can be easily moved around the house. The seat height, at 480mm, is a little higher than normal. It is perfect for taking a break while cooking or working. If you combine this stool with the 'Pinched-leg dining table' (page 130), you can create a useful space-saving table set.

The legs are slender and look like they might be wobbly, but when you sit it feels stable. That's because of the halved joint braces that support the legs. Pinching the bracing between two thin legs can produce strength comparable to that of much sturdier parts. A chisel is used to cut out the slots in the cross-shaped halved joint that connects the legs, but it isn't as complicated as it looks.

DRAWING

Scale = 1/8

Measurements = mm

- Screw in from the front side
- Screw in from the back side
- Brass nail
- Screw direction
  (specified as appropriate)

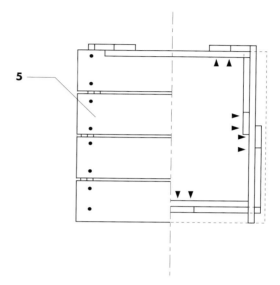

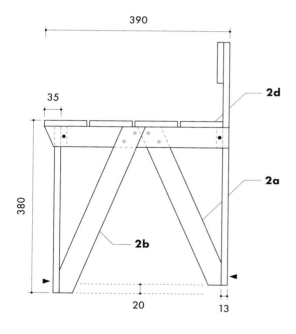

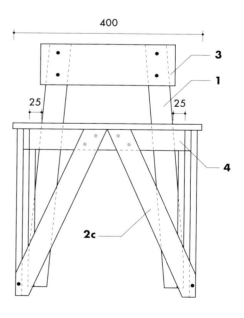

1 Use both a combination square and angle finder to mark out the dimensions. Then, cut. Make sure the lines are marked properly.

2 After you finish processing the materials, sand and chamfer them with a hand plane. The corners should be sanded as they are easily chipped by hand planes.

3 To assemble the frame under the seat (**2d, 4**), verify and mark the mounting positions on the front and rear frame pieces. Align the top edges so they are flush and fasten with screws. (Screws: 35mm)

4 Assemble the four V-shaped legs (**1, 2a, 2b, 2c**). First, drive the screw in until the tip pierces the board. Insert the tip into the other board, and then fasten. (Screws: 35mm)

5 Assemble two sets of symmetrical V-shaped legs (**1, 2a, 2b, 2c**). Check the drawing carefully to make sure that the leg tips don't overlap in the wrong way.

6 Align the top edge of the curtain board with the top edge of the front legs so they are flush. Mark the positions of the legs and the positions for the screws.

7 Place the V-shaped leg so that it touches the centre of the curtain board. Drill pilot holes at the marked positions and then fasten with screws. (Screws: 25mm)

8 The base of both V-shaped legs should be attached to the sides and back of the curtain board. The base of each side and the top of the curtain board should be flush and then screwed together. (Screws: 25mm)

9 Attach the back part of the V-shaped legs symmetrically. Use a ruler, as shown in the photo. Move to a position 25mm away from the edge of the frame and fasten. (Screws: 25mm)

10 Attach the seat plate (**5**) by screwing down the four corners of each piece, one by one. Fasten the screws in one corner and then the opposite.

11 To attach the back plate (**3**), place it against the protruding back legs and determine the screw positions. When fastening the back plate with screws, drive them in a diagonal pattern. (Screws: 25mm)

12 Place the chair on a flat surface and check if there is any rattling. If it wobbles, adjust by sawing or sanding the end of the offending leg down.

04

TRIANGULAR GARDEN CHAIR

TIME 4 hours

LEVEL ●●●○○

This large garden chair is very comfortable. The seat of the chair itself is large enough to hold a cushion, so you can easily sit cross-legged or with something on your lap. It's not just for the garden either, it can also be used in the living room for relaxing and reading. If the seat depth is too deep, you will need to adjust it by placing an extra cushion between the backrest and the middle of your back.

The triangle where the seat and backrest join is a rational structure, which efficiently distributes the force applied to the joint and firmly supports the backrest with the rear legs. The front and rear frame pieces are installed in notches cut out of the front and back legs. This is done to improve rigidity and make the structure more resistant to swaying from side to side. If the chair is to be left outdoors for long periods of time, painting or staining the surface will make it last longer.

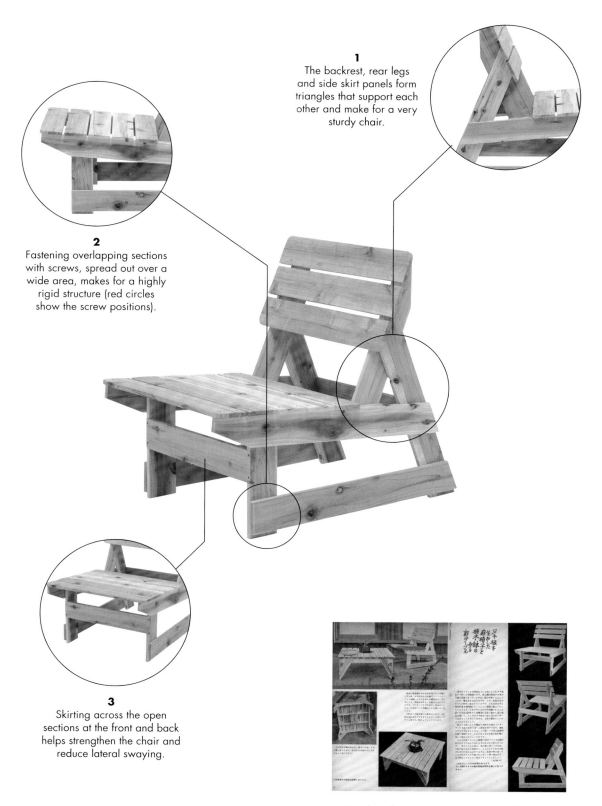

1
The backrest, rear legs and side skirt panels form triangles that support each other and make for a very sturdy chair.

2
Fastening overlapping sections with screws, spread out over a wide area, makes for a highly rigid structure (red circles show the screw positions).

3
Skirting across the open sections at the front and back helps strengthen the chair and reduce lateral swaying.

Garden chair made from rough-cut lumber, from original publication.

PARTS AND MATERIALS

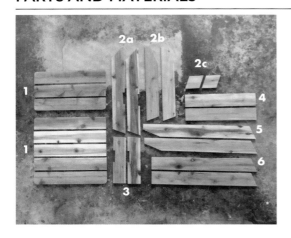

t = thickness
1 t13 x 90 x 525mm: 8 boards
2 t13 x 90x 650mm: 4 boards
3 t13 x 90 x 350mm: 2 boards
4 t13 x 90 x 469mm: 2 boards
5 t13 x 90 x 765mm: 2 boards
6 t13 x 90 x 710mm: 2 boards
The numbered pieces above are referred to
in both the drawings and the instructions.

TOOLS

Double-edged saw, chisel, hammer, clamps, ruler
and tape measure, carpenter's square, combination
square and angle finder, impact driver, screws
(35mm, 25mm), brass nails (35mm) hand planes,
electric sander, sandpaper, wood glue

SIZE OF PARTS

Scale = 1/10
Measurements = mm

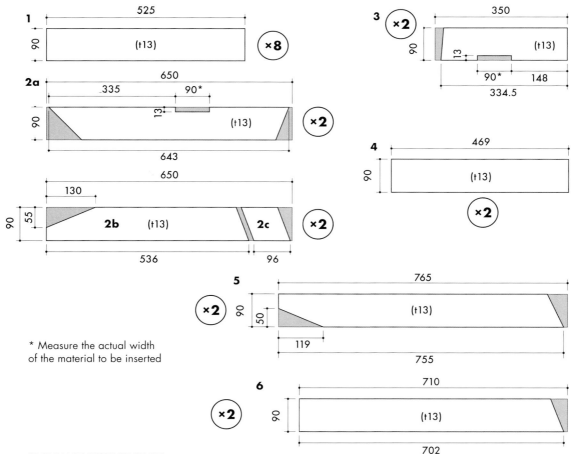

* Measure the actual width
of the material to be inserted

DRAWING

Scale = 1/10

Measurements = mm

- Screw in from the front side
- Screw in from the back side
- Brass nail
- Direction of screws
  (specified as appropriate)

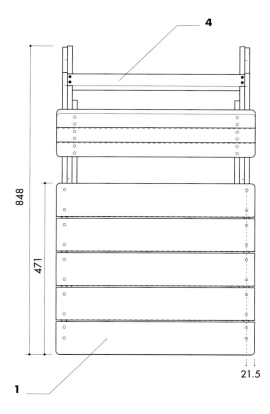

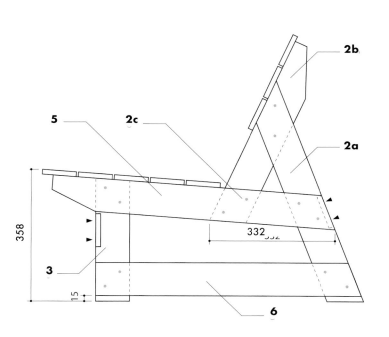

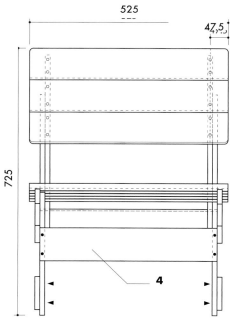

1 Use a combination square and angle finder to mark off the lines and dimensions on the wood pieces. Then cut using a saw.

2 Make incisions for the leg notches (**2a, 3**), using a saw to first cut along the markings, and then make several more cuts to the right depth between the two initial cuts.

3 Slowly cut down to the right depth with a chisel. Then, align the chisel with the marked line and remove material with a hammer.

4 Once cut, sandpaper all the parts and finish the edges with a hand plane. The four corners of the seat boards and back boards should be rounded off smoothly.

5 Assemble the two side frames (**2a, 3, 5, 6**). Screw them while checking the angles of each member with a combination square and angle finder. (Screws: 25mm)

6 To attach spacers (**2c**), check the mounting position of spacer and backrest support (**2b**) on the drawing. Be sure to screw down the spacer first. (Screws: 25mm)

7 Place the backrest support (**2b**) snugly over the spacers and screw in place. Press down firmly while screwing so the components don't shift. (Screws: 25mm)

8 Make sure the skirting (**4**) fits into the notches on the front and back legs. If they don't fit, use a chisel to adjust.

9 If there is any rattling after dry fitting, just straighten the fittings and screw in place while pressing down firmly. Once attached, the whole chair should be solid. (Screws: 35mm)

10 Dry fit the seat board and back board to check positions (**1**). Arrange the boards so that the gaps between them are even. Mark with a pencil. Drill pilot holes in the back boards to make driving in the nails easier.

11 Hold the back boards in place while pressing the chair up against a wall or holding with your feet to keep stable. Hammer in the nails. (Brass nails: 35mm)

12 Place on a flat surface to check for any wobbling. If there are any problems, adjust by sawing or sanding until the chair sits perfectly flat.

BOX-SHAPED BENCH

This chair doubles up as a storage box for use in a living room or a child's room. If you put two or three together and lay a cushion on top, it becomes a compact bench. When you have unexpected guests, you can quickly put away any clutter inside of these chairs. A single chair can also be used in a hallway for removing and putting on shoes, or for storage.

The body is made of 18mm-thick cedar boards. It is sturdily joined with box-jointing. The four corners are fixed with long screws from different directions to create a highly rigid structure. The seat (lid) is made of 5.5mm-thin plywood, but the back side of the plywood is reinforced, so you can sit with peace of mind.

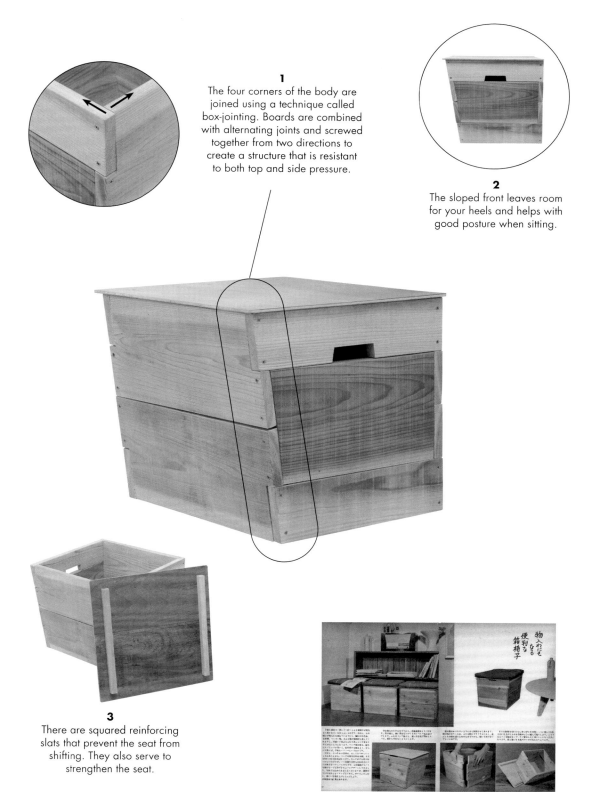

1

The four corners of the body are joined using a technique called box-jointing. Boards are combined with alternating joints and screwed together from two directions to create a structure that is resistant to both top and side pressure.

2

The sloped front leaves room for your heels and helps with good posture when sitting.

3

There are squared reinforcing slats that prevent the seat from shifting. They also serve to strengthen the seat.

Convenient box chair that can also be used for storage, from original publication.

PARTS AND MATERIALS

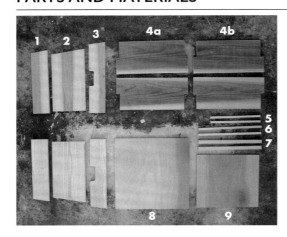

t = thickness
1 t18 x 180 x 370mm: 1 board
2 t18 x 180 x 355mm: 2 boards
3 t18 x 180 x 405mm: 1 board
4 t18 x 180 x 390mm: 4 boards
5 t12 x 12 x 280mm: 2 boards
6 t12 x 12 x 350mm: 2 boards
7 t18 x 18 x 350mm: 2 boards
8 t5.5 x 410 x 410mm: 1 board (plywood)
9 t5.5 x 305 x 350mm: 1 board (plywood)
The numbered pieces above are referred to in both the drawings and the instructions.

TOOLS

Double-edged saw, Azebiki saw, hammer, chisels, clamps, ruler and tape measure, carpenter's square, combination square and angle finder, impact driver, screws (45mm, 25mm, 20mm), hand planes, electric sander, sandpaper, wood glue

SIZE OF PARTS

Scale = 1/10
Measurements = mm

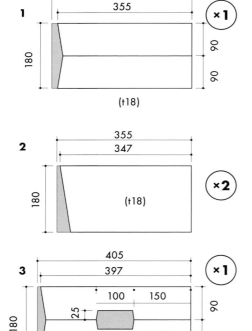

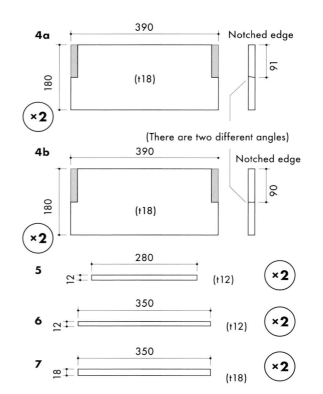

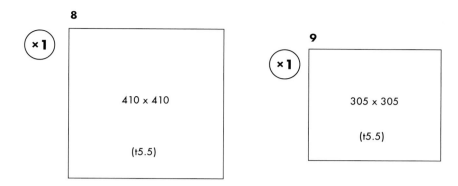

8 ×1

410 x 410

(t5.5)

9 ×1

305 x 305

(t5.5)

DRAWING

Scale = 1/10

Measurements = mm

- ● Screw in from front side
- ● Screw in from back side
- ○ Brass nail
- ▶ Screw direction
  (specified as appropriate)

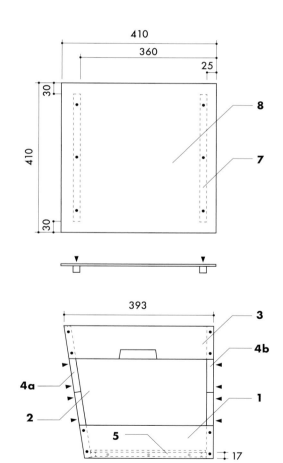

410

360

25

30

410

30

8

7

390

365

9

6

393

3

4b

4a

2

1

5

17

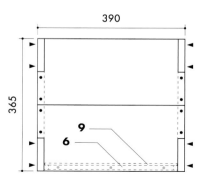

1 Mark and cut all the parts. As you cut, support pieces **1** and **3** with clamps, using your hands to catch the cut-off pieces.

2 To notch the sides for the handles (**3**), first cut in from the edges. Then use an Azebiki saw to begin the base cut. Start in the middle of the mark and gradually lift the saw vertically until you cut through the piece fully.

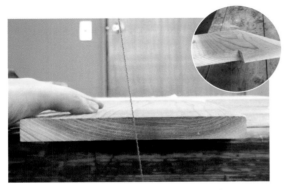

3 Notch out the front and back boards (**4a, 4b**). Note that the face of the front board will be cut at an angle. Use a carpenter's square to mark and cut the correct angle.

4 Once processing is complete, sandpaper all the materials and chamfer edges with hand planes. The ends should be chamfered with sandpaper as they can chip easily.

5 Attach the back and side plates (**1, 2, 3, 4b**). Fasten the screws while holding firmly, so the joints do not separate. (Screws: 45mm)

6 Assemble the components in order from the bottom (**1, 2, 3, 4b**). Carefully tighten the screws while pressing on the pieces firmly with your hand. This will ensure that the back and both sides fit correctly. (Screws: 45mm)

7 Attach the front (**4a**). Your pieces may not be cut at right angles because of machining inaccuracies. Be sure to hold the front piece so that it fits nicely with the sides. (Screws: 45mm)

8 Make holes in the support pieces (**5, 6**). They are thin and easily broken, so they should have pilot holes drilled in them with a countersunk bit.

9 Attach four bottom supports to the inside of the box. Measure and mark the positions so that the supports are at the same height (they can be flush with the bottom if desired). Fasten with screws. (Screws: 25mm)

10 Mark the back side of the lid (seat plate) (**7, 8**). Measure the inside dimensions of the box and mark out the support positions. Also mark the screw positions.

11 Attach supports to back side of the lid (seat plate) (**7, 8**). Drill through the lid using pre-drilled holes in supports as a guide. Countersink the top side holes so that screws will sit properly. Align the supports and fasten with screws while pressing firmly. (Screws: 20mm)

12 Insert the bottom plate until it sits on the attached bottom supports from step 9. If it doesn't fit properly, adjust with sandpaper or a hand plane. Place the lid on the box.

PINCHED-LEG HIGH CHAIR

06

TIME 3.5 hours
LEVEL ●●●○○

This low chair is perfect for babies who are able to sit up. It comes with a removable table that is great for holding food, drinks or little snacks. The height of the seat can be adjusted at the time of construction according to the height of the child. The approximate height range is 80–110cm. The footrest can freely change height and angle, even after installation. It can also be removed when the child gets too big for it.

Children are always active, even when sitting down. That's why this chair is built in such a sturdy way. The legs are pinched and doubled to add strength. Also, when viewed from the side, the legs spread out like a capital 'A' to add stability. The seat and backrest are part of the overall structure and effectively prevent swaying. There are a variety of ingenious features hidden in this very attractive chair.

2

Fastening the tips of the pinched legs with screws applies pressure to the sandwiched parts, thus fixing the parts together more tightly. The height of the seat can be adjusted by taking advantage of the width of the leg gap.

1

The legs close towards the top, like a capital 'A'. That way, even if the child rocks back and forth, the chair will remain stable.

3

The footrest can be removed when the child becomes too big to use it. Once removed, the tips of the front legs can be squeezed together and fastened, thus increasing the strength even more.

*The pinched-leg high chair,
from original publication.*

PARTS AND MATERIALS

t = thickness
1 t13 x 45 x 270mm: 2 boards
2 t13 x 90 x 341mm: 4 boards
3 t13 x 90 x 285mm: 1 board
4 t18 x 18 x 150mm: 2 boards
5 t13 x 90 x 390mm: 2 boards
6 t13 x 45 x 420mm: 8 boards
7 t13 x 45 x 450mm: 2 boards
8 t13 x 45 x 355mm: 2 boards
9 t13 x 45 x 150mm: 2 boards
10 t13 x 45 x 311mm: 1 board
11 t13 x 90 x 311mm: 1 board
The numbered pieces above are referred to
in both the drawings and the instructions.

TOOLS

Double-edged saw, ruler and tape measure,
carpenter's square, combination square and
angle finder, impact driver, right-angle offset tool,
screws (45mm, 25mm, 20mm), hand planes,
electric sander, sandpaper, wood glue

SIZE OF PARTS

Scale = 1/10
Measurements = mm

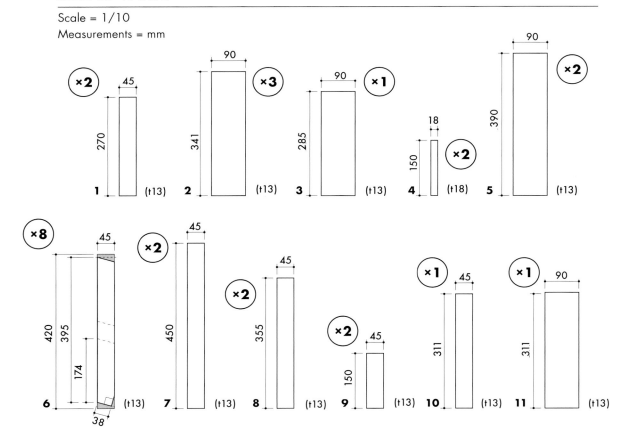

DRAWING

Scale = 1/10
Measurements = mm

- ● Screw in from side
- ● Screw in from back
- ○ Brass nail
- ► Direction of screw
  (specified as appropriate)

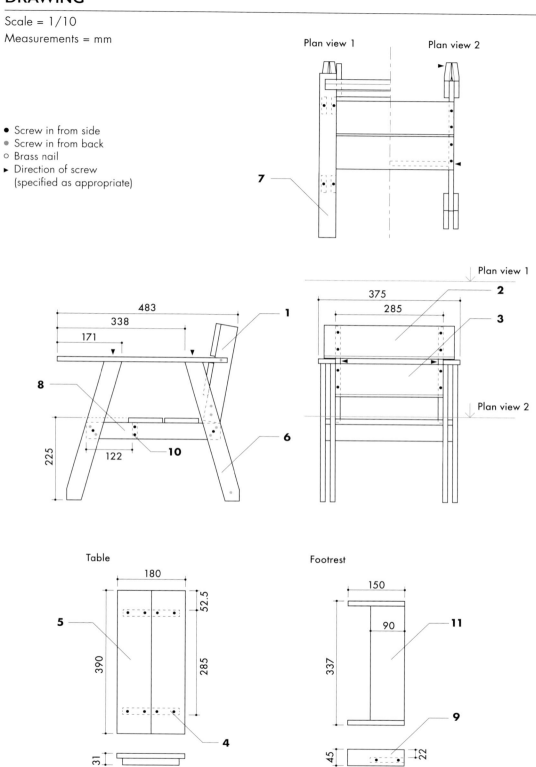

Plan view 1

Plan view 2

7

Plan view 1

483
338
171

1

8

225
122

10

6

375
285

2

3

Plan view 2

Table

180
52.5
285
390
31

5

4

Footrest

150
90
337

11

45
22

9

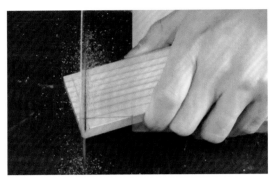

1 Use a carpenter's square and combination square to mark out the dimension lines on the pieces. Cut them with a saw. Make sure all lines are properly marked before cutting.

2 Cross-cut or angle cut the ends with the correct bladed saws. Use your thumb on the side of the saw to steady the blade when cutting.

3 After processing, finish all materials with sandpaper or a hand plane. Chamfer ends with sandpaper as they are prone to chipping. Pointed corners should also be sanded.

4 Check the positions of the legs, armrests and all holes (**6, 7, 8**). Clamp a suitable piece of wood to the bench and use it to level your pieces while dry fitting.

5 Screw together the armrests, legs and bracing (**6, 7, 8**). Attach the bracing (screws: 35mm). Insert a suitable piece of wood when attaching the armrests (screws: 45mm) to maintain the right width all the way along.

6 Assemble the backrest (**1, 2, 3**). Attach the back plates to the risers. Check the position on the drawing and fasten with screws. When fixing the wider board, shift screws so they are fixed along a slight diagonal. (Screws: 35mm)

7 Secure the backrest and legs. Run backrest risers inside of the back legs and the armrests. Adjust to the desired angle and screw in place. (Screws: 25mm)

8 Fasten with screws (**10**). Attach the stabilizer to prevent the legs from spreading. Be sure to align the top edge of the stabilizer with the top edge of each brace. (Screws: 35mm)

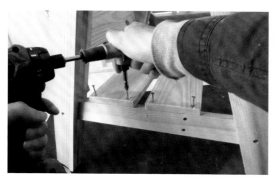

9 Attach the seat plates (**2**). Use a right-angle offset tool to screw in the seat plates. At this point it is easier to leave the screws sticking out. (Screws: 35mm)

10 Put the table together (**4, 5**). The position of the two support bars under the table is determined by measuring the inside dimensions of the armrest. Once you are sure the table will fit, fasten support bars with screws. (Screws: 25mm)

11 Assemble the footrest components (**9, 11**) in a 'U' shape. Determine where to attach the footrest by having the child sit in the chair. Attach the footrest by screwing through from the outside legs. (Screws: 35mm)

12 Close the rear leg ends and fasten to complete. Place on the flattest surface possible and check stability. If there is any wobbling, adjust by sawing or sanding down the leg ends as needed.

V-SHAPED LEG GARDEN BENCH

TIME 4.5 hours
LEVEL ●●●○○

This bench is large enough for three people to sit side by side. If placed in a garden, you can relax and enjoy looking out over the greenery. For garden parties, it can easily be combined with the 'Variable-height table' (page 142) so that you and your guests will all have somewhere to sit while you eat. When used indoors, cushions or blankets can be added to soften its rustic appearance.

In addition to the four corner legs, there is one in the centre so that three adults can sit on the bench at the same time, without it bending. The corner legs are thin and not strong enough on their own, but by joining them in a V-shape and screwing their tips together, they become much stronger and will not rock back and forth. The centre leg is straight, but it is connected front and back with a cross-brace, so there is no danger of it wobbling.

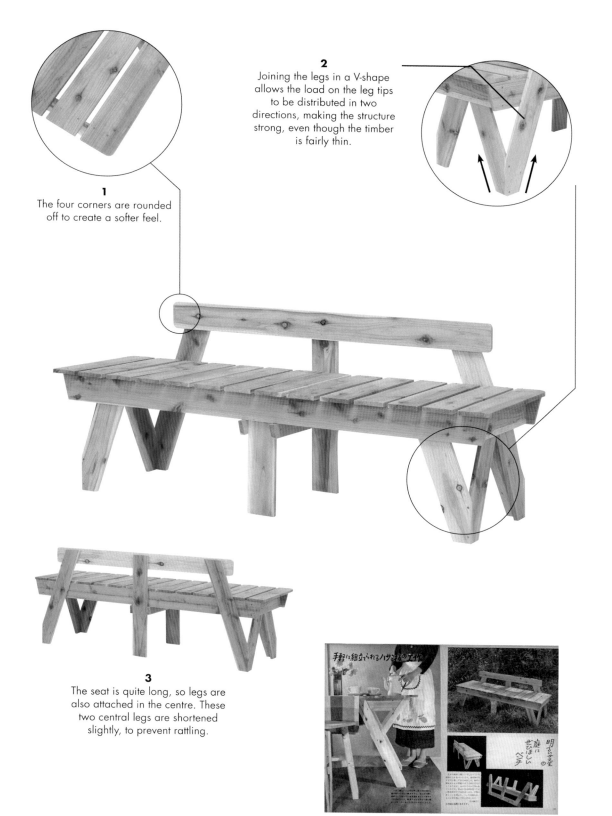

1
The four corners are rounded off to create a softer feel.

2
Joining the legs in a V-shape allows the load on the leg tips to be distributed in two directions, making the structure strong, even though the timber is fairly thin.

3
The seat is quite long, so legs are also attached in the centre. These two central legs are shortened slightly, to prevent rattling.

The garden bench, from original publication.

PARTS AND MATERIALS

t = thickness
1 t13 x 90 x 1080mm: 1 board
2 t13 x 90 x 405mm: 14 boards
3 t13 x 90 x 1400mm: 2 boards
4 t13 x 90 x 450mm: 6 boards
5 t13 x 90 x 650mm: 2 boards
6 t13 x 90 x 560mm: 1 board
7 t13 x 90 x 365mm: 1 board
8 t13 x 90 x 345mm: 2 boards
9 t13 x 45 x 415mm: 2 boards
The numbered pieces above are referred to in both the drawings and the instructions.

TOOLS

Double-edged saw, hammer, clamps, ruler and tape measure, carpenter's square, combination square and angle finder, impact driver, screws (35mm, 25mm), brass nails (35mm, 25mm) hand planes, electric sander, sandpaper, wood glue

SIZE OF PARTS

Scale = 1/10
Measurements = mm

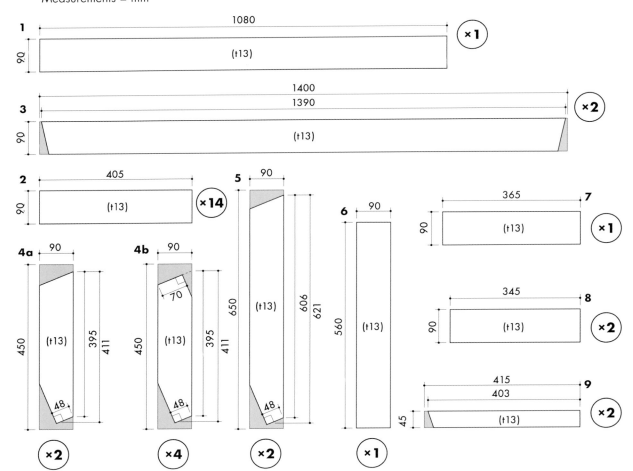

DRAWING

Scale = 1/10
Measurements = mm

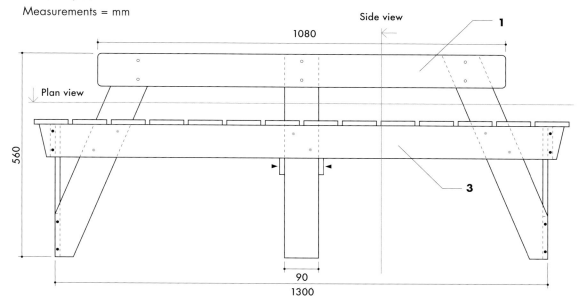

Side view

Plan view

1080

1

3

560

90

1300

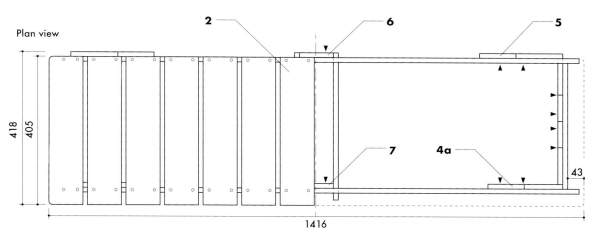

Plan view

2

6

5

418

405

7

4a

43

1416

- Screw in from side
- Screw in from back
- Brass nail
- Direction of screw
  (specified as appropriate)

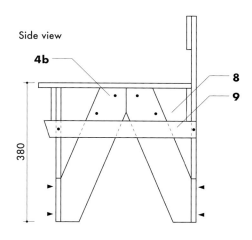

Side view

4b

8

9

380

1 Use a combination square and angle finder to mark out the materials using a pencil. Then use a saw to cut all parts.

2 After cutting the materials, sand and/or plane all pieces. All edges of the backrest and the seat should be rounded nicely.

3 Construct the frame (**3, 8**) by applying glue to the joints. Press down firmly while screwing pieces together so they don't separate. (Screws: 35mm)

4 To put together the V-legs (**4a, 4b, 5**), drive the screws in until the tips just pop out the back of the board. Stick the tip of the screw into the side to be joined, adjust if necessary and then fasten. (Screws: 35mm)

5 Align the top of the frame and front legs so that they are flush. Fasten them with screws. Use two screws at the base of each leg. Be careful not to mistake the left and right sides for each other. (Screws: 25mm)

6 Since the back legs will be fine-tuned in the next step, the base of the back legs are temporarily fixed to the frame, screwed together with a single screw. (Screws: 25mm)

7 Check for wobbling in the main unit by standing it up. If it rattles, adjust the rear legs by moving them around a bit. Fix with screws when there is no rattle.

8 To attach the front and rear centre legs (**6, 7**), centre each leg along the frame and fasten with screws. Make sure that the centre legs are not longer than the left and right legs. This will prevent rattling. (Screws: 25mm)

9 Attach the central brace (**9**) after butting it up against the frame. Make sure everything is level and then screw bracing into centre legs from the side. (Screws: 35mm)

10 Lay out the seat plates (**2**), check their position and then fix with brass nails. Tack nails in all four corners of each seat plate. (Screws: 35mm)

11 To attach the backrest (**1**), lay the unit down to make nailing easier. Find the correct position for the backrest and then hammer in brass nails to secure. (Brass nails: 25mm)

12 Place on a flat surface and check for any wobbling. If there is a rattle, adjust by sawing or sanding the leg ends as needed.

STURDY PORCH BENCH

TIME 3 hours

LEVEL ●●○○○

This simple porch bench is perfect for sitting out on summer evenings. Indoors, it can be placed in a living room corner, or in the hallway so you can sit down when taking off or putting on your shoes. The bench can be used for many purposes. If you have enough space, you can make multiple units and use them to create any layout you like.

All four legs are made of thin cedar and are sandwiched between two boards of the frame. Cross-brace members are added to increase rigidity, so two adults can sit at the same time. The original drawing shows a two-seater bench, but it can be converted to a three-seater by simply extending the seat by another 500mm and adding a leg to the centre of the seat.

1

Legs are tilted inwards to make them resistant to rocking back and forth. The retracted leg ends also have the advantage of preventing stubbed toes.

2

From the side, the legs and brace form a square. This makes for a very strong base. The legs are also sandwiched between two frame boards to strengthen them even more.

3

The ends of the legs are tapered. This design prevents cracking when the unit is lifted, moved and placed back on the ground.

4

Overlapping parts are fastened with two screws each, across the width of the board, resulting in a highly rigid structure.

Rustic bench made only from cedar, from original publication.

PARTS AND MATERIALS

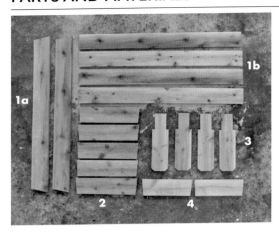

t = thickness
1 t13 x 90 x 900mm: 6 boards
2 t13 x 90 x 350mm: 5 boards
3 t13 x 90 x 315mm: 4 boards
4 t13 x 90 x 280mm: 2 boards
The numbered pieces above are referred to in both the drawings and the instructions.

TOOLS

Double-edged saw, hammer, clamps, ruler and tape measure, carpenter's square, combination square and angle finder, impact driver, screws (35mm, 25mm), brass nails (35mm), hand planes, electric sander, sandpaper, wood glue

SIZE OF PARTS

Scale = 1/10
Measurements = mm

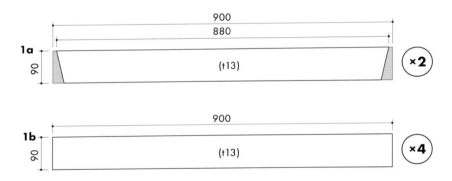

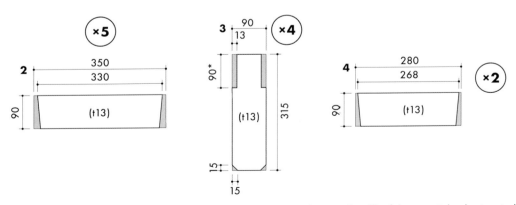

* Measure the actual width of the material to be inserted.

DRAWING

Scale = 1/10

Measurements = mm

- ● Screw in from side
- ● Screw in from back
- ○ Brass nail
- ▶ Direction of screw
  (specified as appropriate)

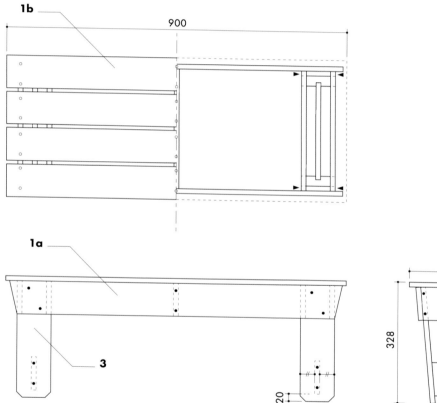

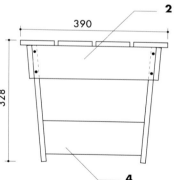

1 Use a combination square and angle finder to mark out the materials. Cut with a saw.

2 Cut notches out of the legs (**3**). Start the saw at a shallow angle. It is easier to notch if you cut horizontally first and then vertically.

3 To cut a notch, start out with the saw at an angle and then gradually raise it until it is vertical. At the end, cut slowly so as not to go over the ink line.

4 After processing, sandpaper all the parts and chamfer them with a plane. The corners should be chamfered with sandpaper because they are easily chipped with a hand plane.

5 Temporarily line up the leg pieces (**2, 3, 4**) without screwing them together. Check that the dimensions are correct. It is also useful to mark the position of the screws for the cross bracing.

6 Attach the upper bracing to the legs. Start with the lower screws. Fix while checking the angle. (Screws: 35mm)

7 Add the lower bracing. Fasten according to the position you laid out in Step 5. (Screws: 25mm)

8 If the legs protrude from the top edge of the frame, shave them down with a hand plane until flush. Shave off a little at a time, using the finest cuts possible.

9 Attach the framing to the legs (**1a**). Align tops of the legs with the frame so that they are flush. Fasten with screws. (Screws: 25mm)

10 Insert the centre bracing (**2**) between the frame pieces at the centre. Fasten with screws from the outside. (Screws: 35mm)

11 Temporarily lay out the seat plates (**1b**). Check their position and then fix to the frame with brass nails. Hammer the nails in each corner for each seat plate. (Brass nails: 35mm)

12 Place the bench on a flat surface and check for any wobbling. If you find any, adjust by sawing or sanding down the leg ends as needed.

V-SHAPED LEG ARMCHAIR

This attractive chair is perfect for relaxing with a book or a cup of coffee. It has both a large seat and armrests, so you can always find a comfortable position. If you want to combine the chair with a table, we recommend the 'V-shaped leg tea table' (page 112). This chair has the largest number of construction steps among those found in this chapter and is more suited to intermediate woodworkers. The shape looks complex, but the structure is quite simple and primarily based on the V-shaped legs we have already seen in other chairs. This chair differs from others in that the legs extend above the seat and serve as supports for the armrests and backrest. If you take a moment to understand the structure first, your work will go more smoothly.

1
By joining the legs in a V-shape, the load on the leg tips is distributed in two directions. This makes the structure strong even when using thin pieces of wood.

2
View of the top panel structure from the back. Since the seat is so wide, a brace has been added in the centre to create a sturdier structure.

3
At first glance, it looks complicated, but the structure is relatively simple: a V-shaped leg is extended to form an armrest.

Chair with sturdy and comfortable armrests, from original publication.

PARTS AND MATERIALS

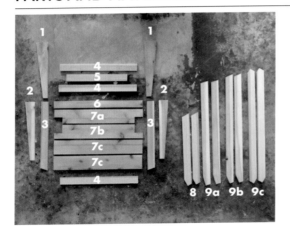

t = thickness
1 t13 × 90 × 350mm: 2 boards
2 t13 × 90 × 360mm: 2 boards
3 t13 × 45 × 450mm: 2 boards
4 t13 × 45 × 466mm: 3 boards
5 t13 × 45 × 379mm: 1 board
6 t13 × 45 × 540mm: 1 board
7 t13 × 90 × 540mm: 4 boards
8 t13 × 45 × 500mm: 2 boards
9 t13 × 45 × 750mm: 6 boards
The numbered pieces above are referred to in both the drawings and the instructions.

TOOLS

Double-edged saw, clamps, ruler and tape measure, carpenter's square, combination square and angle finder, impact driver, screws (35mm, 25mm), brass nail (35mm), hand planes, electric sander, sandpaper, wood glue

SIZE OF PARTS

Scale = 1/10
Measurements = mm

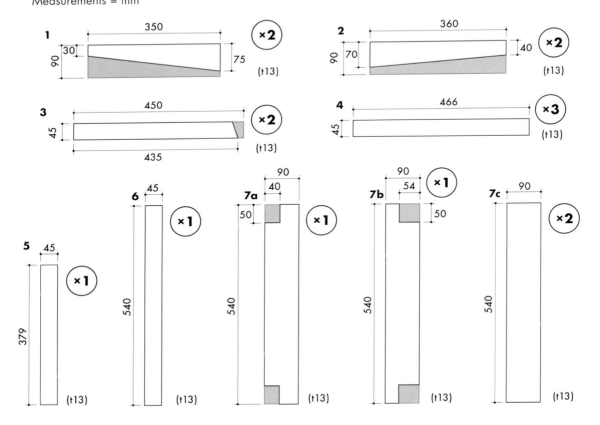

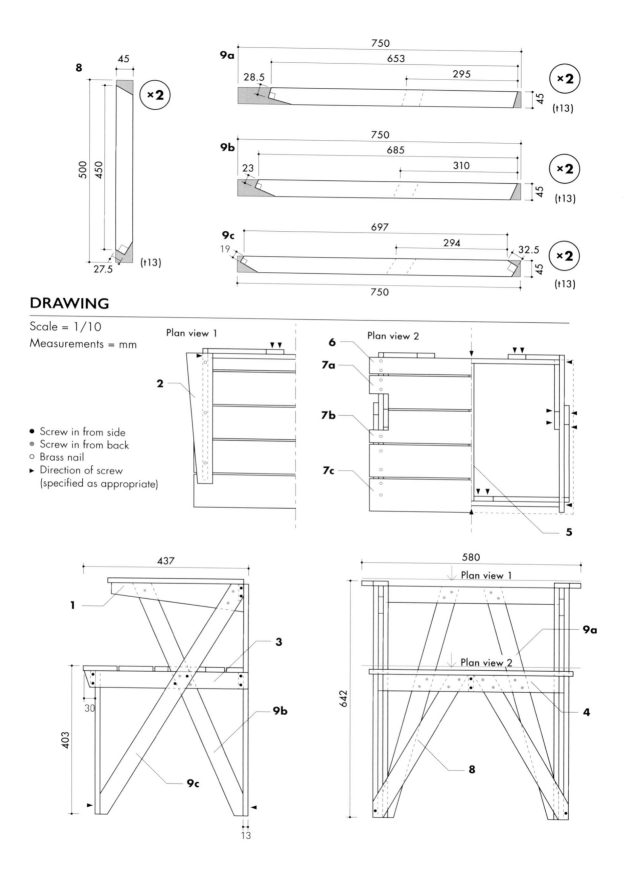

8
45
×2
500
450
(t13)
27.5

9a
750
653
295
28.5
45
×2
(t13)

9b
750
685
310
23
45
×2
(t13)

9c
697
294
19
32.5
45
×2
750
(t13)

DRAWING

Scale = 1/10
Measurements = mm

Plan view 1

2

Plan view 2

6

7a

7b

7c

5

- Screw in from side
- Screw in from back
- ○ Brass nail
- ▶ Direction of screw
  (specified as appropriate)

437

1

3

9b

30

9c

403

13

580

Plan view 1

9a

Plan view 2

4

642

8

1 Use a combination square and angle finder to mark the dimensions and lines on the material with a pencil. Then cut using a saw.

2 Notch the seat board (**7a, 7b**) by cutting horizontally and then vertically. Gradually raise the saw from the beginning of the cut. Raise it vertically a little before the ink line. Cut all the way up to the edge of the line.

3 After processing the materials, sand all parts and chamfer with a hand plane. The corners are easily chipped when using a hand plane, so use sandpaper inside.

4 Now assemble the frame and bracing (**3, 4, 5**). Check the position of the front and rear pieces. Flush up the top edges and screw them together. Centre the brace between the front and rear frame piece and screw it in. (Screws: 35mm)

5 Assemble two sets of symmetrical V-shaped legs (**8, 9a, 9b, 9c**). Check the drawing carefully to make sure the leg tips do not overlap in the wrong way.

6 First, drive screws into the board until the tips barely protrude out the back. Stick the protruding tip into the side to be joined, then fasten. (Screws: 35mm)

7 The board on the front side of the V-shaped legs should be placed and attached so that the top edge of the leg is flush with the top edge of the frame and in contact with the central brace. (Screws: 25mm)

8 Screw the V-shaped legs to the sides and back. Align the frame piece with the marked lines on the legs and screw them in place. (Screws: 25mm)

9 To make the arms (**1, 4**), assemble the back plate and armrest support as shown in the photo. Align the top and back of back panel so that they are flush with each other. Fasten with screws. (Screws: 35mm)

10 Fix the seat boards at each corner with nails (**6, 7a, 7b, 7c**). Drive them in a diagonal pattern. (Brass nails: 35mm)

11 Align the top edge of the V-shaped legs with the top edge of each arm. Fasten them with screws as shown. (Screws: 25mm)

12 Finish by nailing the armrests in place (**2**). Place on a flat surface and check for any wobbling. If it rattles, adjust the leg tips with a saw or sandpaper. (Brass nails: 35mm)

LOW PLYWOOD CHAIR

This chair was originally designed for children, but it is strong enough for adults to use as well. It is perfect for sitting on to take shoes off, or as a work chair when gardening. When combined with the 'V-shaped leg garden table' (page 106) it makes a very useful garden set.

In terms of structure, plywood is a very effective choice. On the seat, it helps to increase the rigidity of the frame, and on the back of the

rear legs, it prevents the chair from racking side to side. Using two pieces of plywood together makes the chair much stronger. Although machining the parts requires precision, their number is small and they are easy to make, so why not try making one of these chairs as a weekend project?

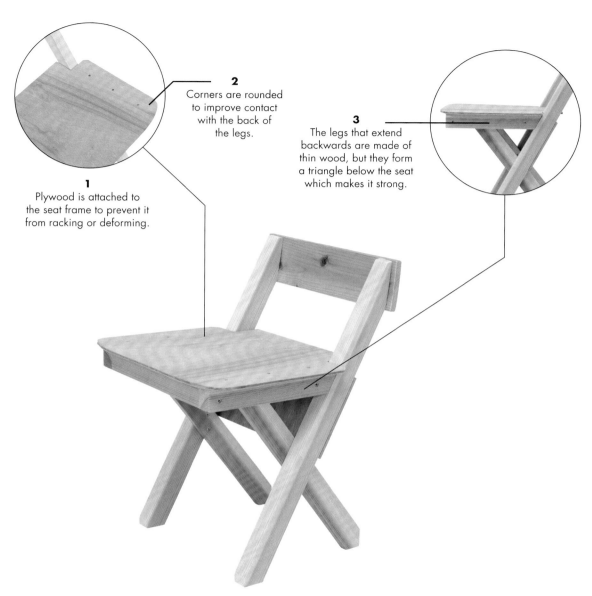

2
Corners are rounded to improve contact with the back of the legs.

1
Plywood is attached to the seat frame to prevent it from racking or deforming.

3
The legs that extend backwards are made of thin wood, but they form a triangle below the seat which makes it strong.

4
A large brace made of plywood is also attached to the back, to prevent swaying.

Use of plywood in children's chairs, from original publication.

PARTS AND MATERIALS

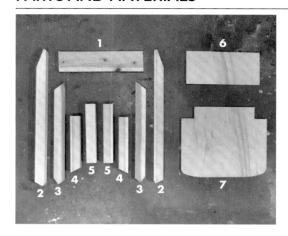

t = thickness
1 t13 x 90 x 360mm: 1 board
2 t30 x 40 x 610mm: 2 pieces
3 t13 x 45 x 470mm: 2 pieces
4 t30 x 40 x 260mm: 2 pieces
5 t30 x 40 x 276mm: 2 pieces
6 t5.5 x 150 x 336mm: 1 board (plywood)
7 t5.5 x 325 x 390mm: 1 board (plywood)
The numbered pieces above are referred to in both the drawings and the instructions.

TOOLS

Double-edged saw, clamps, ruler and tape measure, carpenter's square, combination square and angle finder, impact driver, screws (65mm, 55mm, 35mm), hand planes, electric sander, sandpaper, wood glue

SIZE OF PARTS

S = 1/10
Measurements = mm

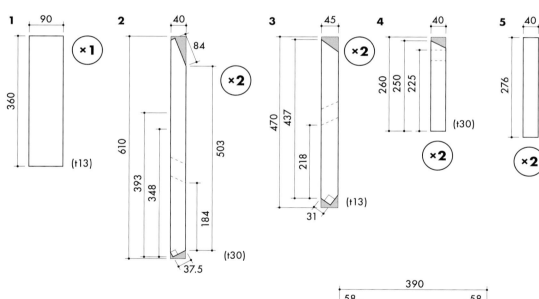

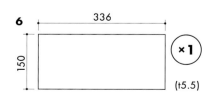

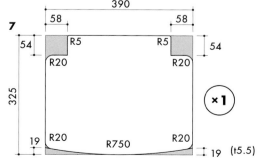

DRAWING

S = 1/8

Measurements = mm

- ● Screw in from side
- ● Screw in from back
- ○ Brass nail
- ▶ Screw direction
  (specified as appropriate)

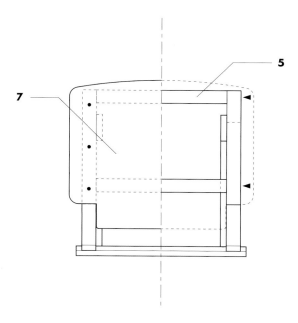

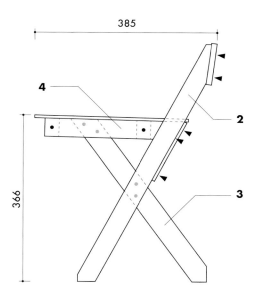

385

366

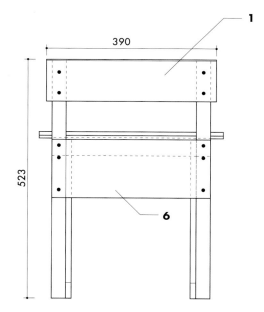

390

523

1 Mark the dimensions and lines on the material using a combination square, angle finder and a pencil. Make sure the lines are properly marked.

2 Use saws horizontally or vertically, as necessary, to cut out the pieces. The joints between the back plate and the rear legs, and between the rear legs and the seat frame, need special care when cutting.

3 To notch the two corners of the frame (**7**), start by laying the saw down, then gradually raise it to a vertical position just before the ink line. Cut right up to the edge of the ink line.

4 After processing, sand all the parts and chamfer them with a hand plane. The corners should be chamfered with sandpaper because they will chip with a hand plane.

5 Assemble the seat frame (**4, 5**) by aligning the parts so that the top edges are flush and fasten with screws. (Screws: 55mm)

6 Fix the front and rear legs in an X-shape (**2, 3**). First, mark out where the parts intersect. Tap the screws until they protrude slightly from the back. Sticking the tip of the screw into the target stops it moving. (Screws: 35mm)

7 Attach the front legs to the seat frame. Determine the position and angle of the screws by placing them on the joint. Pre-drill a hole at the chosen position and fasten while holding the joint firmly. (Screws: 65mm)

8 Attach the seat frame and the rear legs. Place on a flat surface and check for wobbling. If the chair rattles, shift the rear legs until everything is stable. Then, fasten with screws.

9 Place the backrest (**1**) on the back side of the legs and find the correct position. Pre-drill the screw holes first and then fasten it on. (Screws: 35mm)

10 Place the seat plate (**7**) on the frame. Refer to the drawing while marking the screw positions. Pre-drill holes in the seat plate and then fasten the screws. (Screws: 35mm)

11 Attach the plywood back support (**6**) to the back of the rear legs. Place plywood at the intersection of the seat and legs. Screw all four corners. (Screws: 35mm)

12 Place the chair on a flat surface and check for any wobbling. If it rattles, adjust by sawing or sanding the leg ends as necessary.

02 TABLES

Once you have finished making your favourite chair, you may also want to make a table to go with it. This chapter contains nine projects, which can be used in combination with the various chairs introduced in the first chapter. There is even a low Japanese tea table (a *chabudai*) for a Japanese-style room, and a workbench that will come in useful for weekend carpentry.

01 **Round plywood tea table,**
page 94

02 **Pinched-leg side table,**
page 100

03 **V-shaped leg garden table,**
page 106

04 **V-shaped leg tea table,**
page 112

05 **Side table and bookcase,**
page 118

(06) **Writing desk with drawer,**
page 124

(07) **Pinched-leg dining table,**
page 130

(08) **V-shaped leg sawhorse,**
page 136

(09) **Variable-height table,**
page 142

ROUND PLYWOOD TEA TABLE

TIME 3 hours
LEVEL ●●●○○

This Japanese tea table (*chabudai*) has a pleasing design that fits both Japanese and Western-style rooms. Its thin top and slender legs, sticking out at an angle, give it a modern look. The tabletop diameter is 850mm, which is just right for two people. The legs can't be folded, but the table is quite lightweight and can easily be stored away when not in use.

At first glance, it may appear difficult to cut the circular top out of plywood, but if you use a long-bladed saw, with a curved blade, it is surprisingly easy. The plywood top might warp a little as it dries, but that will not interfere with the table's functionality. Be careful not to place your hand, or any heavy objects, at the very edge of the tabletop as this may cause it to tip over.

1
The plywood is only 5.5mm thick. However, by fixing criss-crossed legs to the top panel, it becomes quite strong.

2
Using a long, curved saw blade and advancing the blade slowly, allows you to cut out the circular tabletop without the use of power tools.

3
Fastening the tips of the sandwiched legs with screws applies pressure to the individual parts and they become stronger.

4
The top panel is made up of only three components. The frame pieces criss-cross together and use notches to form cross-lap joints.

Easy-to-build table that uses minimal components, from original publication.

PARTS AND MATERIALS

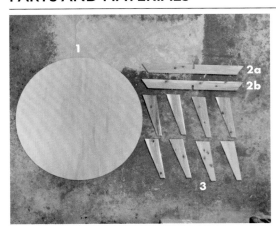

t = thickness
1 t5.5 x 900 x 900mm: 1 board (plywood)
2 t13 x 90 x 680mm: 2 boards
3 t13 x 90 x 330mm: 8 boards
The numbered pieces above are referred to in both the drawings and the instructions.

TOOLS

Double-edged saw, clamps, ruler and tape measure, carpenter's square, combination square and angle finder, impact driver, screws (35mm, 25mm), hand plane, electric sander, sandpaper, glue

PARTS SIZE

Scale = 1/10
Measurements = mm
d = diameter

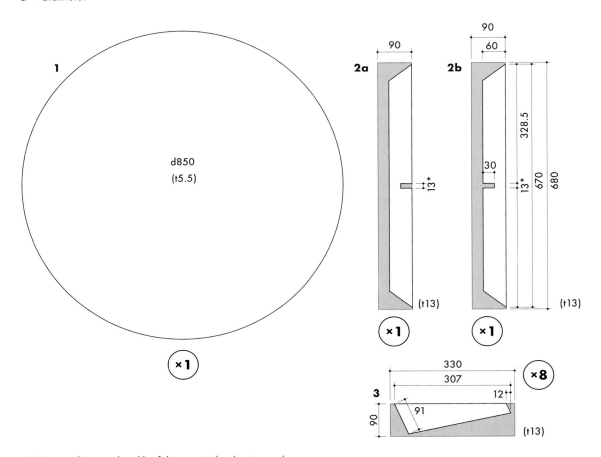

* Measure the actual width of the material to be inserted

DRAWING

Scale = 1/10
Measurements = mm
d = diameter

- Screw in from side
- Screw in from back
- Brass nail
- Screw direction
  (specified as appropriate)

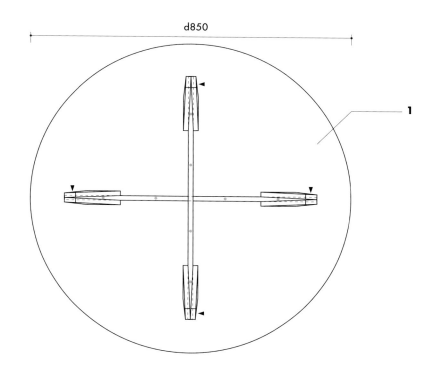

d850

1

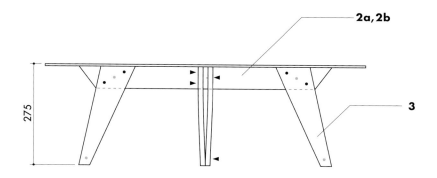

2a, 2b

275

3

1 Mark out the tabletop (**1**) by making a simple compass. Put a screw or nail through one end of a long, thin piece of wood. Measure out the radius and draw the circle while holding the pencil at the correct distance from the screw.

2 Cut out the marked circle (**1**) using a saw with a long blade. Make sure the blade stays perpendicular and then bend it to cut out the circular shape.

3 Use a combination square and angle finder to mark out the legs (**3**). Use a saw to cut the pieces to the right dimensions.

4 Cut the frame pieces (**2a, 2b**). When cutting material lengthwise, use the entire length of the blade to make things easier. Once you have finished cutting, mark out the notches.

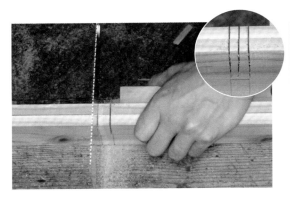

5 Make several cuts for the notches (**2a, 2b**). Use a saw to cut the marked ends. Then, make a cut to carve out some space between those ends.

6 Use a chisel to cut out the notches. Gradually carve out chunks between the end cuts. For the end, align the chisel with the bottom ink line and tap with a mallet to create a nice clean cut.

7 After processing, sand all the parts and chamfer with a hand plane. Corners should be chamfered with sandpaper because they will chip with a hand plane.

8 To attach the legs (**2a, 3**), place the frame piece between the two leg pieces. Align the top edges so that they are flush. Screw together. Squeeze the leg ends together and screw. (Screws: 25mm)

9 Make another set of legs (**2a, 3**). Make sure the notches on both sets of legs fit snugly together. If they do not, adjust with sandpaper or a chisel. (Screws: 25mm)

10 To mark the leg-mounting positions, place the legs, upside-down, on the tabletop and trace their outline. Remove legs and mark the screw positions between traced outlines.

11 Attach the tabletop. First, pre-drill pilot holes at the marked positions. Next, place the tabletop on the legs and drill screws through the pilot holes from the top. (Screws: 35mm)

12 Place the table on a flat surface and check for any wobbling. If it rattles, adjust by sawing or sanding the leg ends as necessary.

PINCHED-LEG SIDE TABLE

This low table has a unique design that is slightly reminiscent of a traditional *torii* gate you would find at a Japanese shrine. If you look closely at the legs, you can see that all parts are assembled diagonally. It is quite compact, measuring just 690 x 360 x 390mm, making it perfect for use as an end table, a stand for audio equipment or for displaying houseplants.

The uniquely shaped legs make a lot of sense. The buttresses protruding from between the legs at an angle are not decorative – they help to distribute the load. At first glance, this table looks complicated, but the process itself is not difficult, with only three components. Precision is required for cutting the notch, so be careful to follow the construction steps closely.

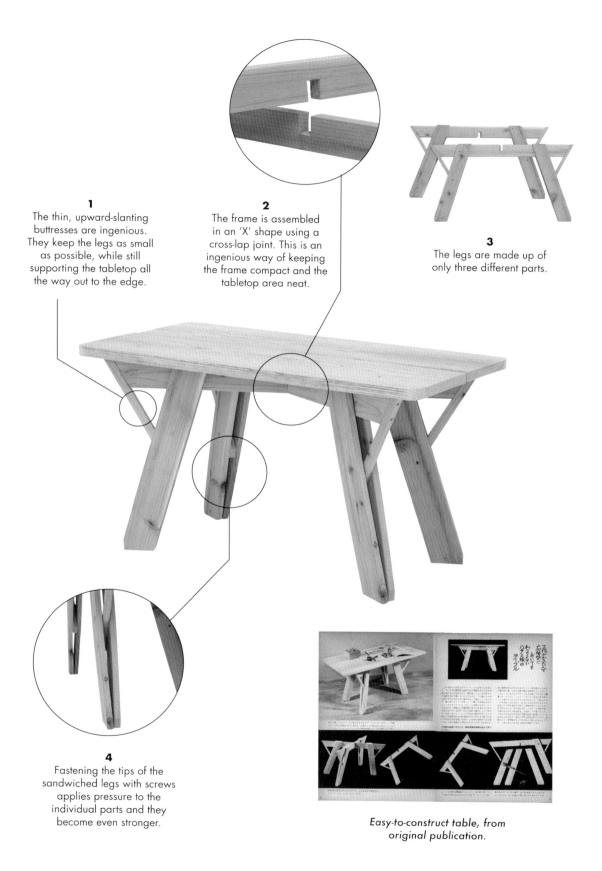

1
The thin, upward-slanting buttresses are ingenious. They keep the legs as small as possible, while still supporting the tabletop all the way out to the edge.

2
The frame is assembled in an 'X' shape using a cross-lap joint. This is an ingenious way of keeping the frame compact and the tabletop area neat.

3
The legs are made up of only three different parts.

4
Fastening the tips of the sandwiched legs with screws applies pressure to the individual parts and they become even stronger.

Easy-to-construct table, from original publication.

PARTS AND MATERIALS

t = thickness
1 t18 x 180 x 690mm: 2 boards
2 t13 x 90 x 660mm: 2 boards
3 t15 x 15 x 275mm: 4 boards
4 t13 x 90 x 420mm: 8 boards
The numbered pieces above are referred to
in both the drawings and the instructions.

TOOLS

Double-edged saw, clamps, ruler and tape
measure, carpenter's square, combination square
and angle finder, impact driver, screws (45mm,
35mm, 25mm), corrugated nails, hand plane,
electric sander, sandpaper, glue

SIZE OF PARTS

Scale = 1/10
Measurements = mm

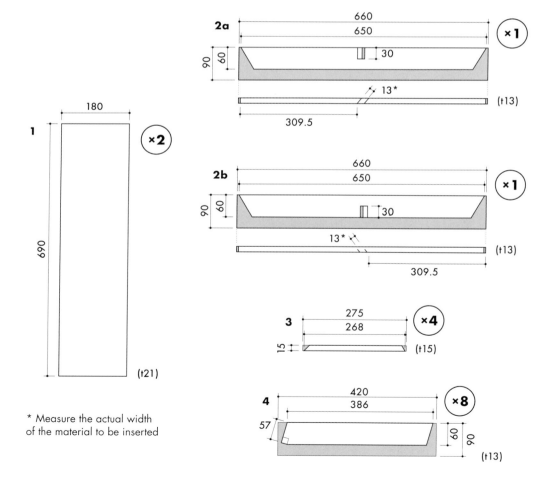

* Measure the actual width
of the material to be inserted

DRAWING

Scale = 1/18

Measurements = mm

- ● Screw in from side
- ● Screw in from back
- ○ Brass nail
- ► Screw direction
  (specified as appropriate)

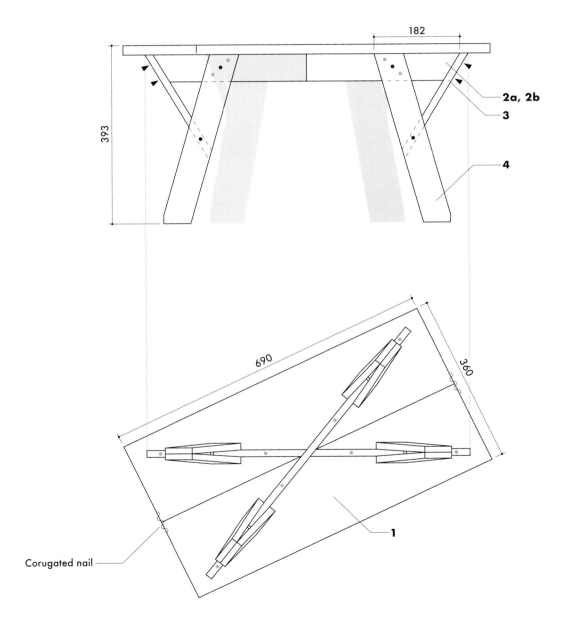

182

2a, 2b

3

4

393

690

360

Corugated nail

1

1 Use a combination square and angle finder for the measurements. Firmly pencil in the markings for all pieces. Cut with a saw.

2 Mark out the notches (**2a, 2b**) using an angle finder to mark the outer edge of the notch (see inset). Balance the frame piece on top and line up with the mark. Pencil off its thickness. Then, use the angle finder to project lines downward.

3 To cut the notches, first, use a saw to carefully cut the ends. Then make another cut between them.

4 Chisel out the notches, gradually carving out the material between the lines. They are at an angle, so be careful with the chisel angle.

5 After processing, sand all parts and chamfer with a hand plane. The corners should be chamfered with sandpaper because they will chip with a hand plane.

6 Pre-drill the holes (**3**). Use a countersink bit to drill holes in buttress pieces. Pre-drilled hole positions should be marked to match the buttress positions on the frame.

7 Attach the supports to the frame (**2a, 2b, 3**). The board is quite thin so hold it firmly and then carefully set the screws. (Screws: 35mm)

8 Make two sets of legs (**4**). Sandwich the frame and buttress pieces between two leg pieces. Drill holes, and then fasten with screws. Cut off any protruding material. (Screws: 35mm)

9 Hold the leg pieces (**4**) down firmly at the ends and screw them in place, keeping leg tips close together. (Screws: 25mm)

10 Position the legs upside-down on the tabletop and trace their outline. Mark the screw positions after removing them.

11 To attach the tabletop, pre-drill the marked screw positions. Next, place the tabletop onto the legs and screw in from the top of the table. (Screws: 35mm)

12 Place the table on a flat surface and check for any wobbling. If it rattles, adjust by sawing or sanding the leg ends as necessary.

V-SHAPED LEG GARDEN TABLE

TIME 4 hours
LEVEL ●●○○○

This low table can be used indoors, or outdoors on a warm day. The size of the tabletop is 750 x 750mm square. The hollow in the centre was designed to display flowers, but you can also put in a small Japanese grill (*shichirin*) with a diameter of 180mm, or less, and enjoy a *yakiniku* party. If you don't want to sit on the ground, you can comfortably combine the table with the 'Low plywood chair' (page 86).

The construction of this table is relatively simple compared to the other tables in this chapter. If you look at the legs, you will see a triangular combination that extends directly down and out diagonally from the tabletop. This is called a brace structure and it helps to improve leg strength. This design also has the advantage of preventing the legs from leaving marks when placed on *tatami* mats or carpets.

1
View of tabletop from rear.
The two centre pieces
increase the strength of the
entire structure.

2
The central hollow can
hold a small flowerpot or
a Japanese grill. (Diameter
less than 180mm.)

3
The diagonal legs serve as braces (left).
The straight legs prevent leaning to
either side (right) and the V-shaped
assembly of the two parts resist swaying
from side to side.

*Garden table with
flowerpot, from original
publication.*

PARTS AND MATERIALS

t = thickness
1 t13 x 90 x 638mm: 4 boards
2 t13 x 90 x 750mm: 6 boards
3 t13 x 90 x 320mm: 4 boards
4 t13 x 90 x 230mm: 2 boards
5 t13 x 90 x 664mm: 2 boards
6 t13 x 90 x 400mm: 4 boards
7 t13 x 90 x 280mm: 4 boards
The numbered pieces above are referred to in both the drawings and the instructions.

TOOLS

Double-edged saw, clamps, ruler and tape measure, carpenter's square, combination square and angle finder, impact driver, screws (35mm, 25mm), brass nails (35mm), hand plane, electric sander, sandpaper, glue

SIZE OF PARTS

Scale = 1/10
Measurements = mm

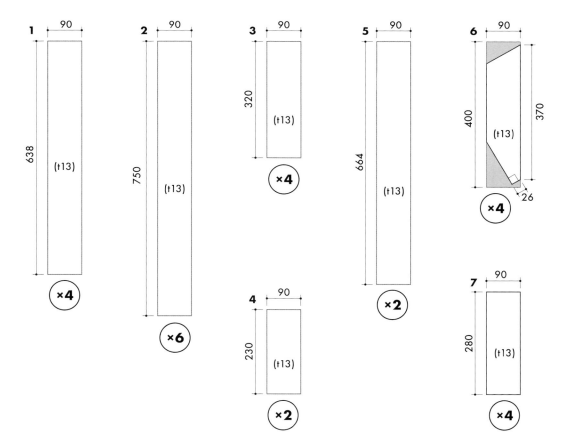

DRAWING

Scale = 1/10

Measurements = mm

- • Screw in from side
- • Screw in from back
- ○ Brass nail
- ▶ Screw direction
  (specified as appropriate)

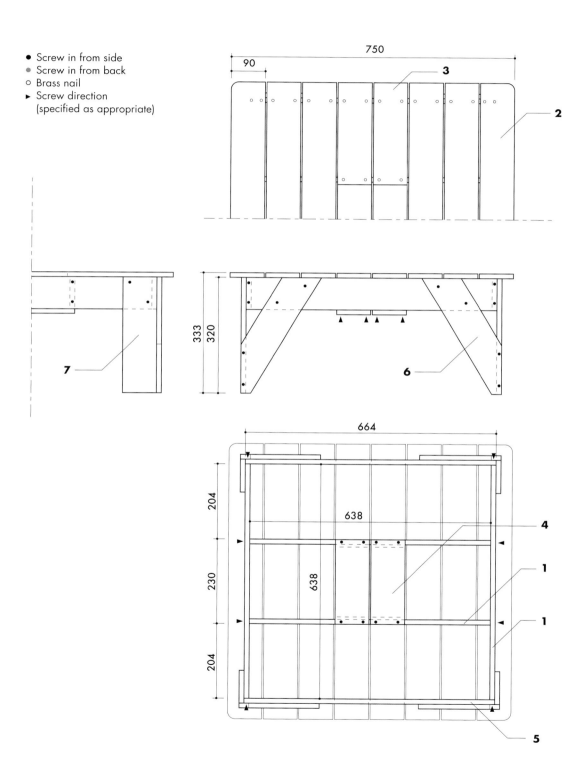

1 Use a combination square and angle finder and firmly mark the measurements with a pencil. Cut out all parts with a saw.

2 Use a saw to roughly cut off the corners on the top boards (**2**). Then gradually make smaller cuts to round them down. Once they are round, use sandpaper to smooth them.

3 After processing, sand all the parts and chamfer with a hand plane. The corners should be chamfered with sandpaper because they will chip with a hand plane.

4 Assemble the frame by making two L-shaped pieces first, before joining them together. To do this, join parts (**1**) and (**5**). Drill pilot holes in the frame and then fasten the screws. This will keep the board from splitting. (Screws: 35mm)

5 Attach the bracing (**1**) to the inside of the frame. Check the position on the drawing and mark. Press the parts together and fasten. Take care not to let the joints separate. (Screws: 35mm)

6 Assemble two pairs of symmetrical V-shaped legs (**3, 6**). Check the drawing carefully to make sure the leg tips do not overlap in the wrong way. (Screws: 35mm)

1

The frame firmly supports the table's edge and prevents deformation, even if heavy objects are placed at the corners.

2

By joining the legs in a V-shape, the load on the leg tips is distributed in two directions. This makes them strong even when using thin boards.

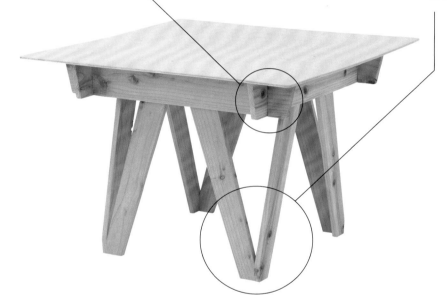

3

Cutting the ends of the frame at an angle helps the entire piece look sharp and clean.

Neat triangular-legged tea table, from original publication.

PARTS AND MATERIALS

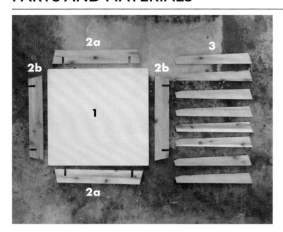

t = thickness
1 t5.5 x 630 x 630mm: 1 board (plywood)
2 t13 x 90 x 580mm: 4 boards
3 t13 x 90 x 500mm: 8 boards
The numbered pieces above are referred to in both the drawings and the instructions.

TOOLS

Double-edged saw, clamps, ruler and tape measure, carpenter's square, combination square and angle finder, impact driver, screws (35mm, 25mm), hand plane, electric sander, sandpaper, glue

SIZE OF PARTS

Scale = 1/10
Measurements = mm

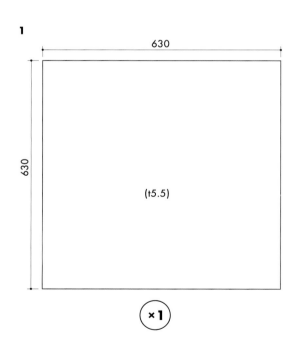

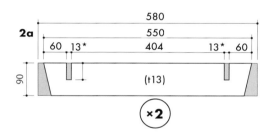

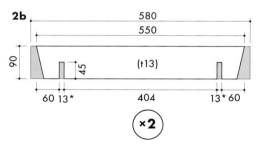

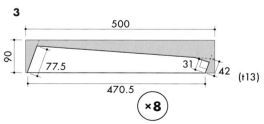

* Measure the actual width of the material to be inserted

DRAWING

Scale = 1/8
Measurements = mm

- ● Screw in from side
- ● Screw in from back
- ○ Brass nail
- ► Screw direction
  (specified as appropriate)

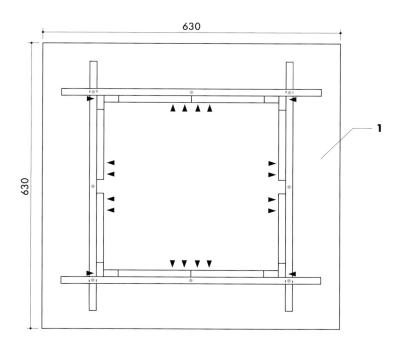

1

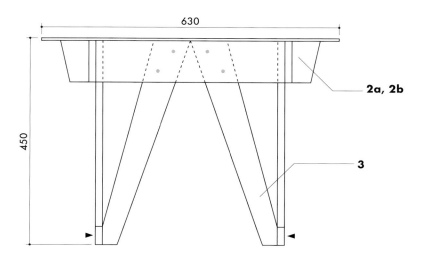

2a, 2b

3

1 Use a combination square and angle finder to make measurements and firmly mark the lines with a pencil. Cut with a saw.

2 Make the notch incisions (**2a, 2b**). Cut at both ends of the marked notches. You can also make an extra cut in the middle. This will make subsequent chiselling easier.

3 If the material is too thin to be clamped, place a suitable piece of wood on the workbench and then clamp firmly.

4 Gradually chisel out the notches between the lines (**2a, 2b**). At the end, align the chisel precisely on the line. Tap the chisel with a hammer, to remove remaining wood.

5 Cut the leg pieces (**3**). When splitting material vertically, use the entire length of the saw blade to make cutting easier.

6 Form four sets of V-shaped legs (**3**). Drive the screw in until the tip protrudes from the back of the first piece. Stick the screw tip into the other part and fasten. (Screws: 35mm)

7 Check the drawing carefully to make sure the leg tips do not overlap the wrong way.

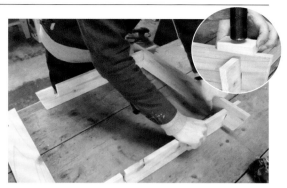

8 Assemble the frame in a box shape (**2a, 2b**). Combine the notched pieces. If the fit is too tight, use a piece of wood as a spacer and tap lightly and evenly on the sides.

9 Attach the V-shaped legs to the frame. Check the drawing for the correct positions and align the top edge of the frame and the legs. Fasten with screws from the inside. (Screws: 25mm)

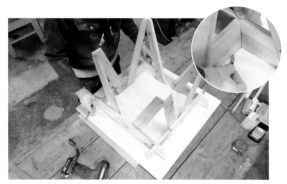

10 Place the legs upside-down on the tabletop to mark the leg-mounting positions. Trace the outline with a pencil. Mark the screw positions along the centre line (relative to outline) of the frame.

11 Attach the tabletop by pre-drilling pilot holes at the marked screw positions. Place the tabletop onto the legs and fasten the screws from the top using the pilot holes as a guide. (Screws: 45mm)

12 Place the table on a flat surface and check for any wobbling. If it rattles, adjust by sawing or sanding the leg ends as necessary.

SIDE TABLE AND BOOKCASE

TIME 3.5 hours
LEVEL ●●○○○

This is a small plywood side table with excellent storage capacity. Highly recommended for book lovers, both sides of the lower compartment are shelves that can hold a collection of, even large-sized, books. They can be stored at an angle for easy access and spine visibility. The top panel also makes a lovely tea table to rest your cup while you read.

If you fill the shelves with books, this case will become quite heavy. However, the main structure is made with thick boards assembled in an L-shape, so it is quite strong. The legs, which appear to be light, are firmly fixed to the back of the shelves with screws, so they can handle the load without too much trouble. The leg parts are small and complex in shape, so be sure to secure them with clamps when cutting.

1

Mounting the L-shaped shelves in a slightly tilted position allows the books to fit better. It also makes them less likely to fall off the shelves when lifting or moving the table.

2

Since the L-shaped shelves themselves are the main structure, the side panels are deliberately made of thin plywood to create a sense of lightness.

3

Handles cut into the plywood make it easy to move around.

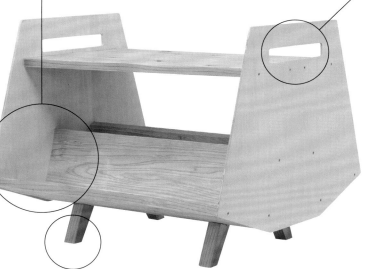

4

The legs may look flimsy but attaching them directly to the shelf makes for a structure that can withstand a significant load.

A side table and bookshelf for any relaxing space, from original publication.

PARTS AND MATERIALS

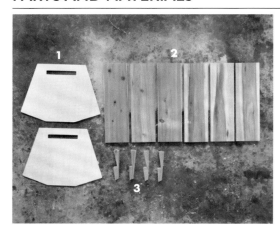

t = thickness
1 t5.5 x 445 x 580mm: 2 boards (plywood)
2 t18 x 180 x 600mm: 6 boards
3 t30 x 40 x 240mm: 4 boards
The numbered pieces above are referred to in both the drawings and the instructions.

TOOLS

Double-edged saw, craft saw, clamps, ruler and tape measure, carpenter's square, combination square and angle finder, impact driver, screws (45mm, 25mm), corrugated nails, hand plane, electric sander, sandpaper, glue

SIZE OF PARTS

Scale = 1/8
Measurements = mm

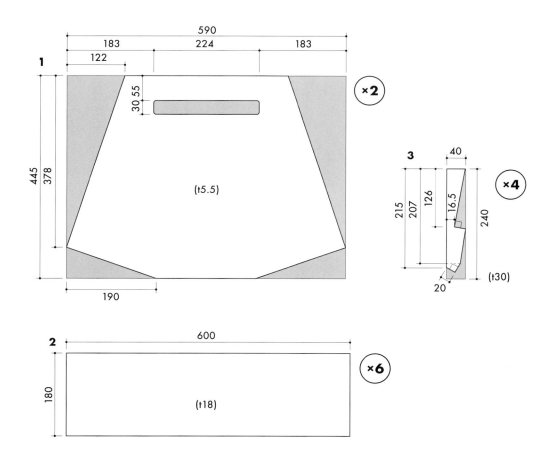

DRAWING

Scale = 1/6

Measurements = mm

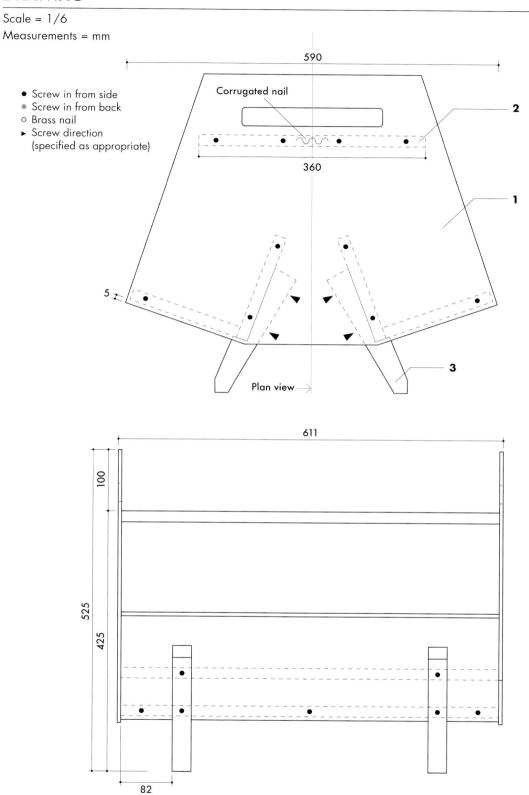

- Screw in from side
- Screw in from back
- Brass nail
- Screw direction (specified as appropriate)

590

Corrugated nail

2

360

1

5

3

Plan view →

611

100

525

425

82

1 On the plywood, with pencil, mark out any outlines, position of tabletop and the handle.

2 Cut out four legs (**3**) using cross-cut and ripping saw blades. The pieces are too small to hold down by hand, so use a clamp to fix firmly in place.

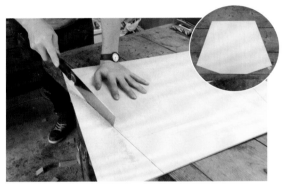

3 Cut out the side panels (**1**). When cutting plywood, lay the saw down as much as possible for easier cutting. At the end of the cut, support the wood with your hand to prevent breakage.

4 Drill a hole, with a 10mm bit, at each corner of the pencil-marked handle holes.

5 Start sawing from one drilled hole and cut along the marked lines. Once the handles are cut, finish the surface with a chisel and/or sandpaper.

6 After processing, sand all the parts and chamfer with a hand plane. The corners should be chamfered with sandpaper because they will chip with a hand plane.

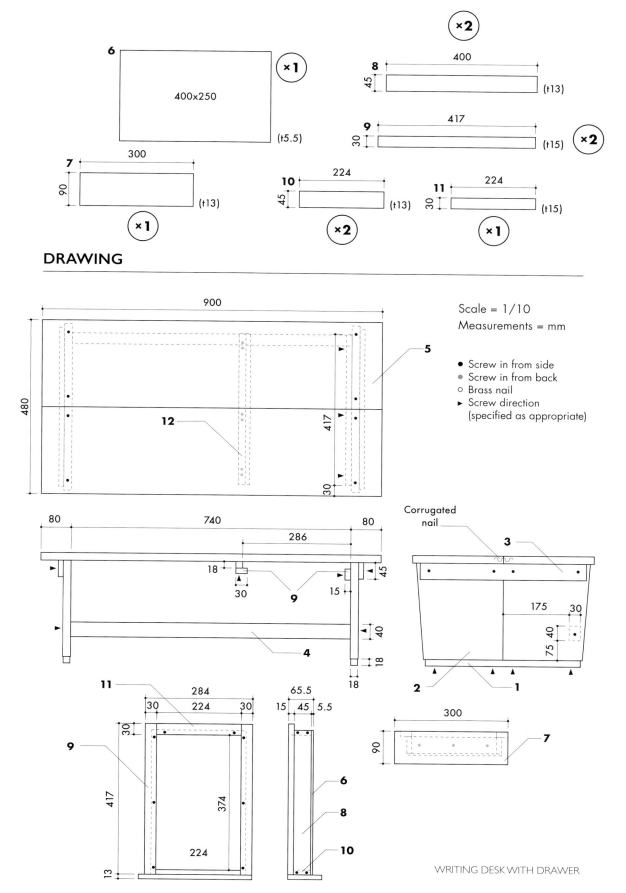

6 400x250 ×1 (t5.5)

×2
8 400 45 (t13)

9 417 30 ×2 (t15)

7 300 90 ×1 (t13)

10 224 45 ×2 (t13)

11 224 30 ×1 (t15)

DRAWING

900

480

5

417

30

12

Scale = 1/10
Measurements = mm

- Screw in from side
- Screw in from back
○ Brass nail
► Screw direction
(specified as appropriate)

80 740 80

286

18

30

9

15

45

40

18

18

4

Corrugated nail

3

175 30

75 40

2 1

Corrugated nail

11 284

30 224 30

65.5

15 45 5.5

300

90

7

9

417

374

6

8

224

13

10

1 Cut one side of each board to be joined together for the legs (**2**) at a very slight angle. Next, butt together and hammer in corrugated nails to connect the two boards.

2 Attach the square bottom supports (**1**) to the leg pieces with screws. Sink the screw heads to prevent floor damage. (Screws: 35mm)

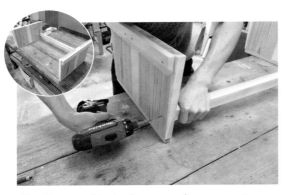

3 To assemble the legs, attach support pieces along the top edge (**3**) and then connect the legs with the brace (**4**). Check the brace position on the drawing. (Screws: 35mm, 45mm)

4 Attach the two tabletop panels (**5**) together with corrugated nails. Place the tabletop onto the legs, check positioning on the drawing and drill pilot holes with a countersink bit. Fasten with screws. (Screws: 45mm)

5 To make the drawer frame (**8, 10**), align the top edges of all four side boards so they are flush. Screw them together. (Screws: 25mm)

6 Align the bottom piece of the drawer (**6**) with the frame and fasten with screws. Fasten screws in a criss-cross pattern. (Screws: 25mm)

7 Align the brim pieces (**9, 11**) with the inside of the drawer so they are flush. Screw the brim to three sides of the drawer. (Screws: 25mm)

8 Screw on the drawer front plate (**7**) from inside. Check the mounting position on the drawing. (Screws: 25mm)

9 To attach the runner to the inside of the leg, place part (**12**) against the top panel as a spacer and position part (**9**) along it. Check the depth of the mounting position on the drawing. Attach part (**9**) with screws. (Screws: 35mm)

10 Create an L-shaped railing by combining the remaining part (**9**) and (**12**) in an L-shape and fasten with screws. (Screws: 25mm)

11 Attach the L-shaped railing to the underside of the tabletop. Temporarily place the drawer and railing in position. Fix the railing at 2mm from that position. The drawer front has been removed in the photo. (Screws: 45mm)

12 Place the desk on a flat surface and check for any wobbling. If it rattles, adjust by sawing or sanding the leg ends as necessary.

PINCHED-LEG DINING TABLE

07

TIME 5 hours
LEVEL ●●●○○

This table is the largest in this chapter. It is 1350mm wide. If you use it in combination with the 'Stool with pinched legs' (page 38), you can create a complete dining set for two people. The tabletop is only 660mm wide, which is quite slim, so it can be placed even in very narrow kitchens. The diagonal legs look beautiful, but some people are concerned about its stability and strength. This piece has a combination of pinched and triangular legs that are strong enough to hold the 1350mm tabletop. The back of the tabletop has five pieces of bracing to prevent deflection. There may be a small amount of shaking during use, but rest assured that it will not break.

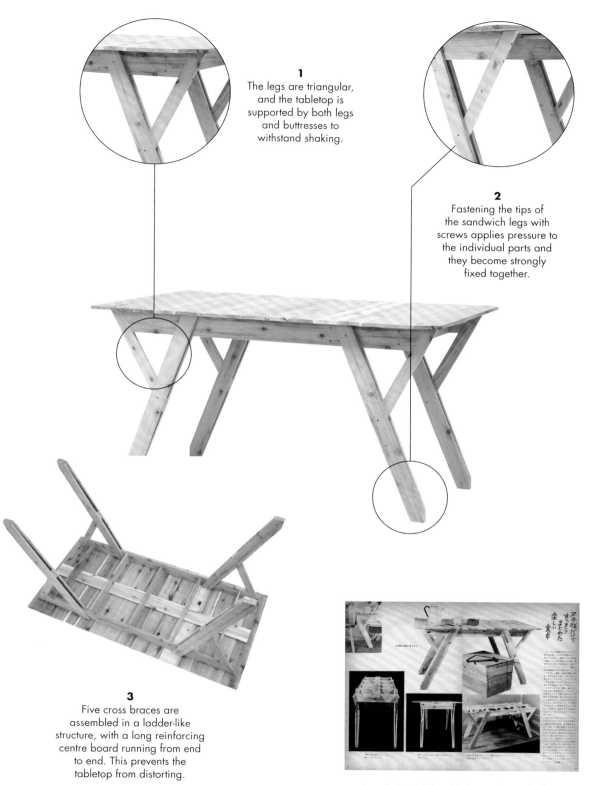

1
The legs are triangular, and the tabletop is supported by both legs and buttresses to withstand shaking.

2
Fastening the tips of the sandwich legs with screws applies pressure to the individual parts and they become strongly fixed together.

3
Five cross braces are assembled in a ladder-like structure, with a long reinforcing centre board running from end to end. This prevents the tabletop from distorting.

Fun dining table with batten boards, from original publication.

PARTS AND MATERIALS

t = thickness
1 t13 x 90 x 1220mm: 2 boards
2 t13 x 90 x 660mm: 15 boards
3 t13 x 90 x 1280mm: 1 board
4 t13 x 45 x 475mm: 4 boards
5 t13 x 90 x 484mm: 5 boards
6 t13 x 90 x 785mm: 8 boards
The numbered pieces above are referred to in both the drawings and the instructions.

TOOLS

Double-edged saw, clamps, ruler and tape measure, carpenter's square, combination square and angle finder, impact driver, screws (60mm, 35mm, 25mm), brass nails (35mm), hand plane, electric sander, sandpaper, glue

SIZE OF PARTS

Scale = 1/10
Measurements = mm

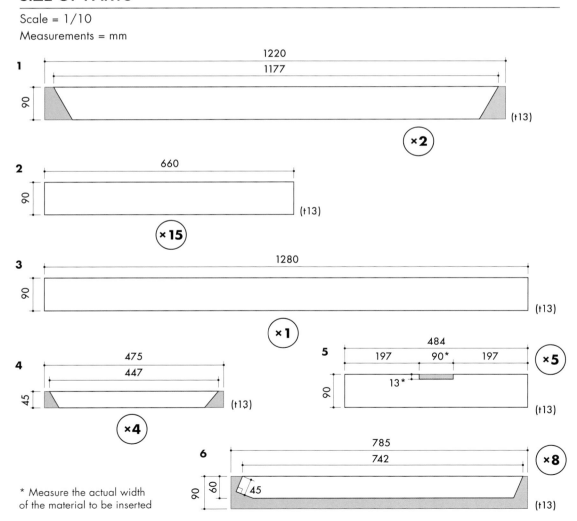

* Measure the actual width of the material to be inserted

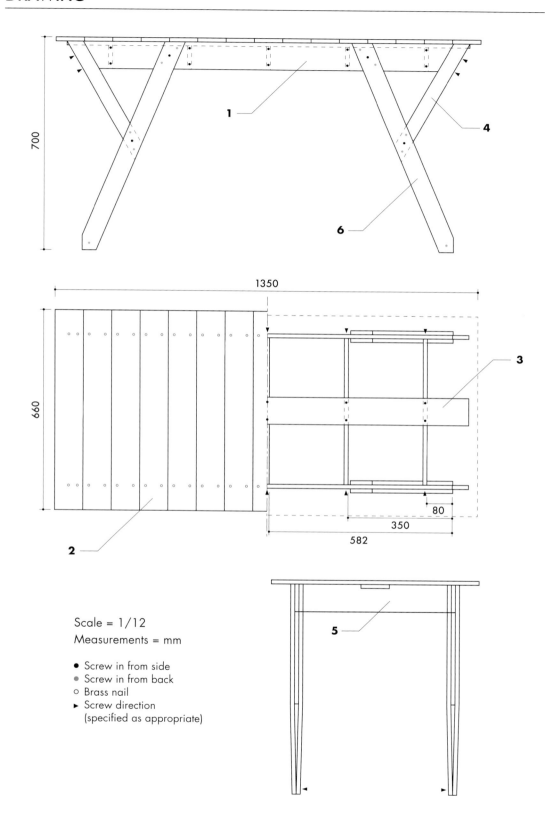

700

1350

660

3

2

80

350

582

Scale = 1/12
Measurements = mm

• Screw in from side
• Screw in from back
○ Brass nail
► Screw direction
(specified as appropriate)

1

4

6

5

1 Mark and process all the parts with a saw. Use a combination square and angle finder to measure and pencil in the markings.

2 Use a saw to cut both ends of the notches (**5**). Then make interior relief cuts. It is more efficient to put several pieces together and fix with clamps for processing.

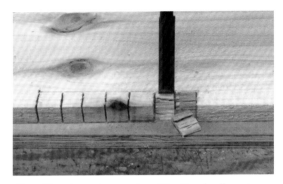

3 Chisel out the notches (**5**). Gradually cut down to the marked lines. At the end, align the chisel with the line and tap with a hammer to remove the final chunks of wood.

4 After processing, sand all the parts and chamfer with a hand plane. The corners should be chamfered with sandpaper because they will chip with a hand plane.

5 Drill holes in the bottom of the diagonal posts (**4**). Use a countersink bit to drill holes in the parts to be attached to the frame. Pilot hole positions should be marked as needed. Align the material with mounting positions on the frame.

6 Attach the diagonal posts to the frame (**1, 4**). The boards are thin, so be sure to hold them firmly and carefully while fastening the screws. (Screws: 60mm)

7 Assemble the sandwiched legs (**6**). Place the frame and the diagonal posts between two leg pieces. Drill pilot holes and then fasten with screws. Tightly close the leg ends by hand and then with screws. (Screws: 25mm)

8 Attach the bracing to the frame (**5**). Place the bracing so that the notched part is facing up to the tabletop. Fasten with screws. Check the position of the bracing on the drawing. (Screws: 35mm)

9 After matching up the bracing positions, connect them to the frame. It is best to fasten both end pieces first, and then fasten the centre pieces. This will prevent shifting. (Screws: 35mm)

10 Lay the centre piece inside the notches in the bracing (**3**). Fasten it to the bracing with two screws each. (Screws: 35mm)

11 Place the tabletop boards onto the frame (**2**). After checking their positions, nail and fix them, starting with the centre board and working outwards. (Brass nails: 35mm)

12 Place the table on a flat surface and check for any wobbling. If it rattles, adjust by sawing or sanding the leg ends as necessary.

V-SHAPED LEG SAWHORSE

The sawhorse is a simple stand on which to place a project, for example, a simple worktable when two are positioned with a tabletop piece. They are very convenient because they don't take up much space and can be moved around easily. The legs are made of thin boards, 45mm wide, whose overlap creates a beautiful silhouette. When not in use, sawhorses can be stacked one on top of each other for easy storage.

The V-shaped legs efficiently distribute load to each leg while the central A-shaped legs resist swaying and provide stability. Sawhorses can be pushed from both the front and back, and either side. The process used for making the base that supports the saddle and makes up the trapezoidal shape can be a bit difficult, so this project received a higher rating for difficulty.

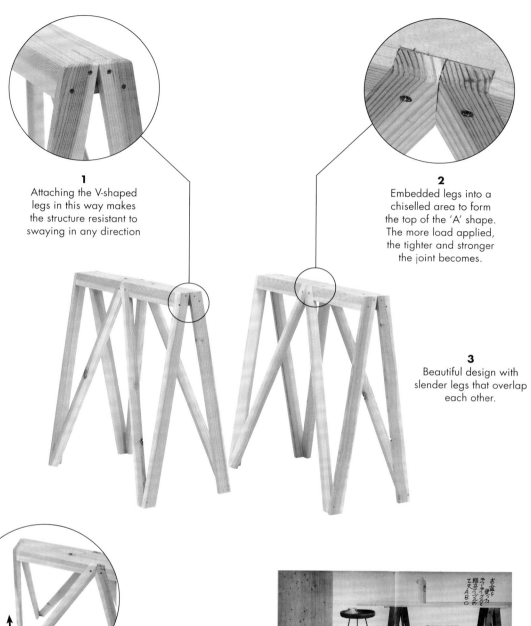

1
Attaching the V-shaped legs in this way makes the structure resistant to swaying in any direction

2
Embedded legs into a chiselled area to form the top of the 'A' shape. The more load applied, the tighter and stronger the joint becomes.

3
Beautiful design with slender legs that overlap each other.

4
Joining legs in a 'V' shape loads them in two directions, thus making the structure stronger, even when using thin boards.

Using sawhorses for tea tables or worktables, from original publication.

PARTS AND MATERIALS

t = thickness
1 t45 x 120 x 630mm: 1 board
2 t13 x 45 x 700mm: 4 boards
3 t13 x 45 x 750mm: 4 boards
The numbered pieces above are referred to in both the drawings and the instructions.

TOOLS

Double-edged saw, clamps, ruler and tape measure, carpenter's square, combination square and angle finder, impact driver, screws (50mm, 40mm), hand plane, electric sander, sandpaper, glue

SIZE OF PARTS

Scale = 1/10
Measurements = mm

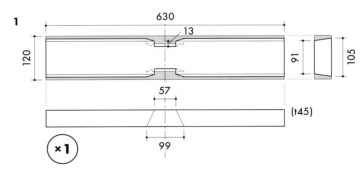

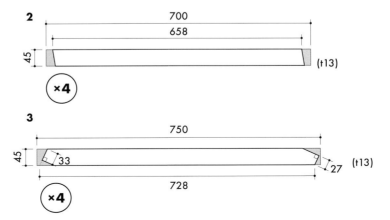

DRAWING

Scale = 1/10

Measurements = mm

- Screw in from side
- Screw in from back
- Brass nail
- Screw direction
  (specified as appropriate)

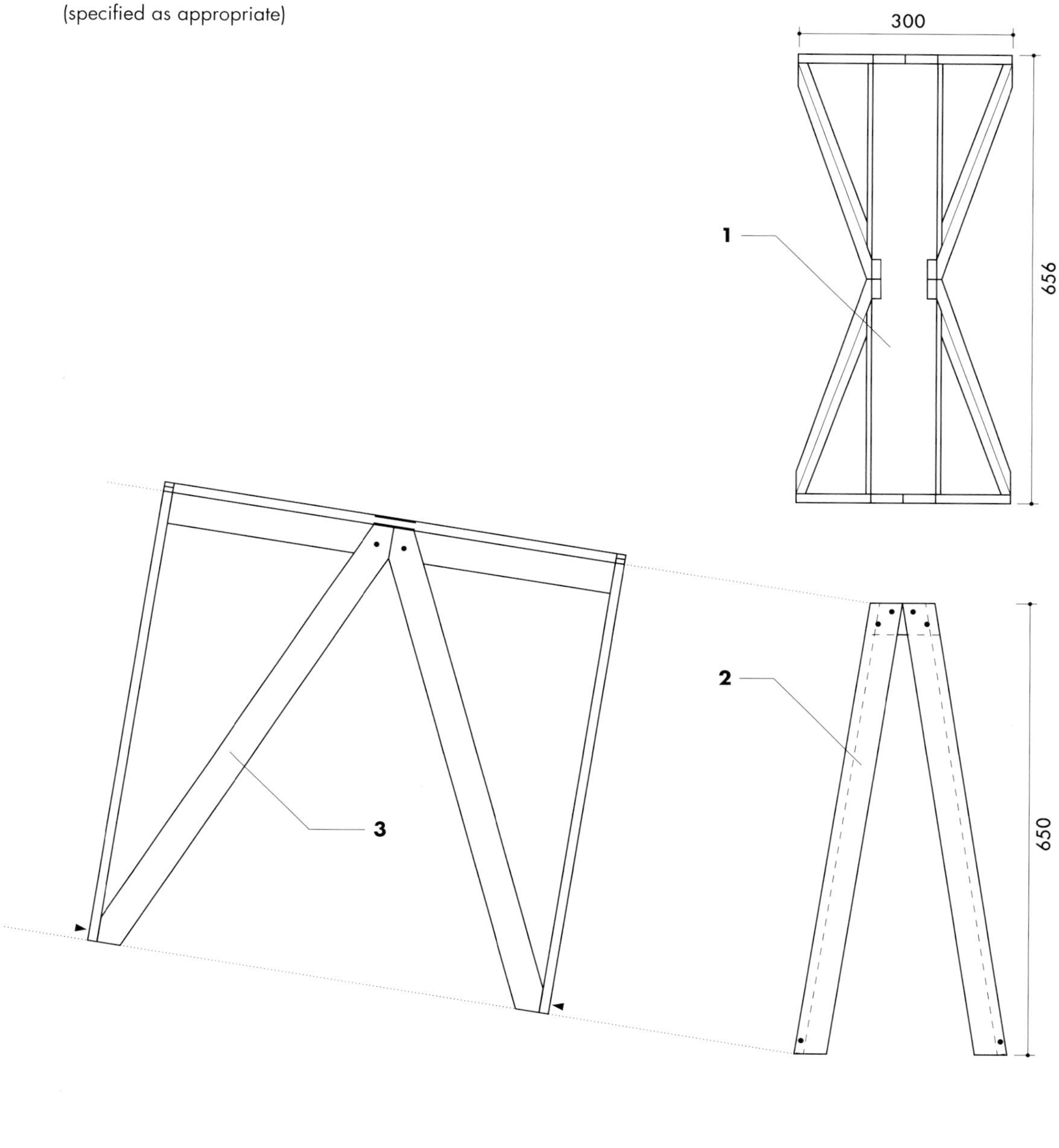

1

2

3

300

656

650

1 Mark all the measurements on the parts and process with a saw. Make sure to mark all the way to the back of the wood, especially the cut-out sections.

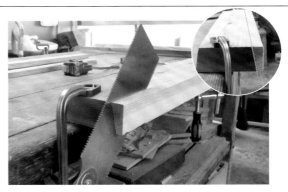

2 Cut piece (**1**) into a trapezoidal shape by tilting the saw blade at an angle to match the marked lines, as you would for straight sawing. Remain conscious of the saw blade alignment, pencil line and centre line.

3 Remove the saw after cutting one side (as shown in inset pic 2). Then, turn the piece around, insert the saw again and cut to the end while moving your body backwards.

4 Make initial diagonal cuts for the notches (**1**). Re-mark the area and make several more cuts. If you make a group of fine cuts between the diagonals, it is easier to finish off the notch.

5 Chisel gradually into the back line of the notches. Outer portions of the notch are at an angle, so take care.

6 Use an angle finder set at the correct angle from the drawing. Place it on the chipped-out surface to make sure it is flat. Use a chisel to clean out any rough areas.

7 Adjust the leg ends (**3**) to fit the notched area in piece (**1**). Make sure both legs fit together in the cut-out area. If they don't fit, adjust the leg ends by shaving with a hand plane.

8 The leg end angles should allow the tips to align with the top edge of the notched area. Fit the legs and fasten with screws. (Screws: 40mm)

9 Attach the remaining legs (**2**). Align the top edges and sides so that they are flush with each other and fasten. Fasten them at two points to prevent rotation. (Screws: 50mm)

10 Close the V-shaped leg tips by screwing the ends together. Screw them while holding firmly, to prevent shifting. (Screws: 40mm)

11 Trim off any protruding edges on the leg corners with a hand plane. Gradually shave down protrusions until there is no bump.

12 Place the sawhorse on a flat surface and check for any wobbling. If it rattles, adjust by sawing or sanding the leg ends as necessary.

VARIABLE-HEIGHT TABLE

This pedestal table is designed to be used with a thick plywood top. When used as a workbench or desk, the pedestals are arranged vertically. If you want to use it as a low table, lay the pedestals on their sides and place the tabletop on them. When using the low side of the pedestals, the table height is somewhat akin to a coffee table (450mm). You could even use this lower version as a bench.

The pedestals are made by simply assembling square pieces into rectangular shapes, so even beginners can complete this project. Even though their construction is simple, these pedestals are strong. At the contact points (each vertex), three square pieces cross and are screwed together simultaneously from three separate directions. This makes the pedestals resistant to both vertical and horizontal swaying. They are stable even with a heavy tabletop on them.

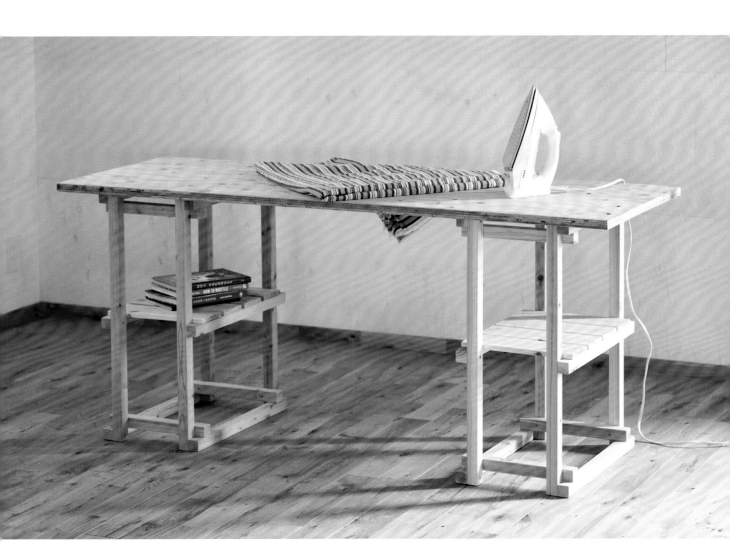

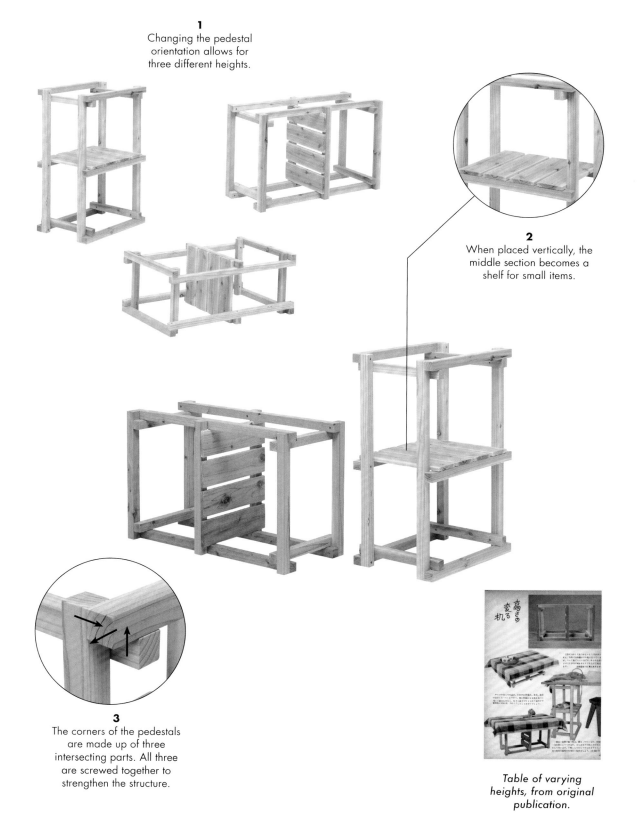

1
Changing the pedestal orientation allows for three different heights.

2
When placed vertically, the middle section becomes a shelf for small items.

3
The corners of the pedestals are made up of three intersecting parts. All three are screwed together to strengthen the structure.

Table of varying heights, from original publication.

PARTS AND MATERIALS

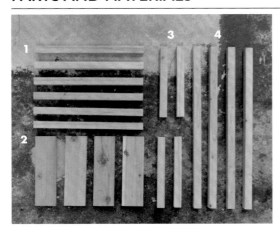

t = thickness
1 t30 x 30 x 450mm: 6 boards
2 t13 x 90 x 300mm: 4 boards
3 t30 x 30 x 300mm: 4 boards
4 t30 x 30 x 690mm: 4 boards
The numbered pieces above are referred to
in both the drawings and the instructions.

TOOLS

Ruler and tape measure, carpenter's square,
combination square, impact driver, screws
(50mm), brass nails (35mm), hand plane, electric
sander, sandpaper, glue

SIZE OF PARTS

Scale = 1/10
Measurements = mm

×6

1
450
30
(t30)

2
300
×4
90
(t13)

3
300
×4
30
(t30)

4
690
30
(t30)
×4

DRAWING

Scale = 1/10

Measurements = mm

- ● Screw in from side
- ● Screw in from back
- ○ Brass nail
- ► Screw direction
  (specified as appropriate)

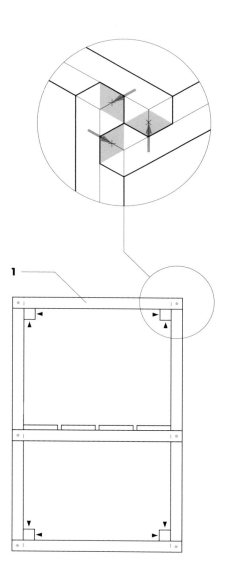

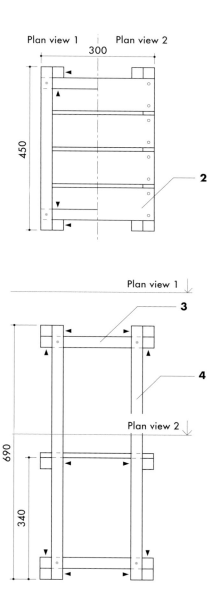

1 Mark, measure and cut all the components. After processing, sand all the parts and chamfer with a hand plane.

2 If you chamfer the edges and corners with a hand plane they may crack or chip. They should be finished using sandpaper.

3 Use a countersink bit to make pre-drilled holes in the frame joints. If the board is only 30mm thick, the screws may not follow the grain without the pre-drilled holes.

4 Use a guide to fix the screw positions. To create even joints, you can use a smooth plate or a flat piece of wood as a jig to accurately align the surfaces.

5 Make two frames in the shape of a window frame (**1, 4**). After pre-drilling, apply glue to the joints and fasten. Check the position of the central square on the drawing. (Screws: 50mm)

6 Once the frame is assembled, use a square to check for right angles. If it is distorted, correct by manipulating with your hands until the frame is square.

③ **Slim display shelves,**
page 164

⑤ **Open-back shoe rack,**
page 176

④ **Simple umbrella stand,**
page 170

STACKABLE BOOKSHELF

This bookcase uses an ingenious system that allows separate shelves to be stacked up like blocks, up to four high, to increase storage capacity. The shelves hold books up to 28cm tall, so they are perfect for organizing children's picture books and magazines. You can also use this unit as decorative shelving in many other areas of your home.

To prevent the shelves from falling over, the sides are designed to slot together. If you look closely at the joint, you can see that there are three boards that are designed to alternately overlap each other, thus preventing shifting, not only back-to-front but also side-to-side. This design has high levels of functionality using only a small number of parts.

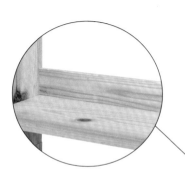

1
The thick shelving and backing board are combined in an 'L' shape to prevent deflection under load.

2
The sides are made up of three boards, two rectangular and one arrow-shaped. The arrow-shaped board prevents rocking front-to-back, while the overlapping 'claws' of the three plates prevent rocking.

3
Up to four shelves can be stacked up one on top of the other. The length of the unit doesn't have to be exactly as shown in the drawing, you can adjust measurements slightly to suit your needs.

The bookshelf from original publication.

PARTS AND MATERIALS

t = thickness
1 t13 x 90 x 300mm: 4 boards
2 t13 x 90 x 350mm: 2 boards
3 t21 x 210 x 750mm: 1 board
4 t13 x 90 x 750mm: 1 board
The numbered pieces above are referred to
in both the drawings and the instructions.

TOOLS

Double-edged saw, hammer, clamps, ruler and
tape measure, carpenter's square, combination
square and angle finder, impact driver, screws
(45mm, 35mm, 25mm), hand planes, electric
sander, sandpaper, glue.

SIZE OF PARTS

Scale =1/8
Measurements = mm

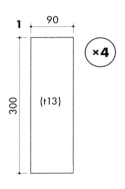

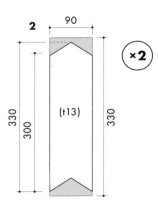

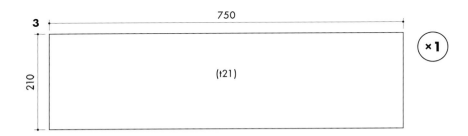

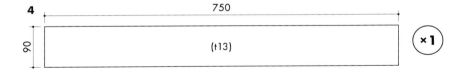

DRAWING

Scale=1/8

Measurements = mm

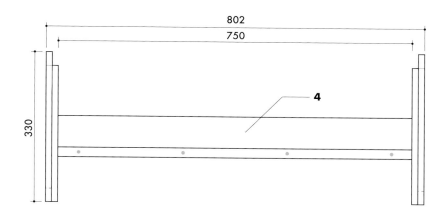

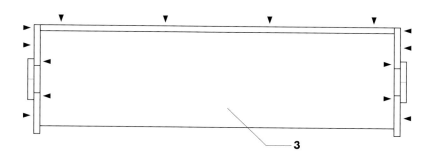

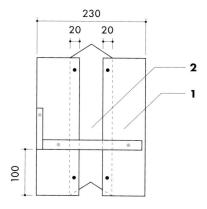

● Screw in from side
● Screw in from back
○ Brass nail
► Screw direction
  (specified as appropriate)

1 Use a ruler, combination square, angle finder and pencil to measure and mark out all the parts.

2 Use an angle finder to mark out the arrow shape (**2**). By keeping the position on your angle finder, the same angles can be marked in multiple places.

3 Use a cross-cut blade to cut a point on one end of the piece (**2**). Make sure these cuts are exact, as they will be important when stacking the shelves later on.

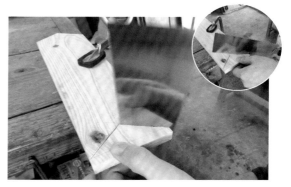

4 For the indented end on piece (**2**), start with your saw at a shallow angle and then gradually increase the angle so that it is completely vertical at the point.

5 After processing, sandpaper all the parts and chamfer with a hand plane. The corners should be chamfered with sandpaper because they are easily chipped with a hand plane.

6 Align the shelf pieces (**3**, **4**) in an L-shape. Fasten the screws in the order of right edge, left edge and centre to prevent any shifting. (Screws: 35mm)

7 Assemble the side panels (**1**, **2**). Mark the areas where the boards will overlap. (Screws: 25mm)

8 Use a square piece of wood at the base of the pieces to align their bottom edges. Align the side boards with the marked lines, press down firmly and fasten with screws. (Screws: 25mm)

9 Mark the positions on the side panels where the shelves will be installed. Use a square to mark lines that are parallel to the bottom edge of the panels.

10 Place a shelf along the marked lines on one of the side panels and fasten with screws. The shelves are easier to assemble standing up, as shown. (Screws: 45mm)

11 Fasten the side panel to the other side with screws in the same way, while aligning it properly with the marked lines. (Screws: 45mm)

12 When you stack multiple units, check the side panel overlap very carefully.

SHELVES WITH STRING DETAIL

This wall-mounted display shelf is made with minimum parts. Using hemp string for the front support reduces its angular appearance. It can easily be installed in a small space, like a bathroom. The shelf depth is relatively small (around 150mm) and not really suitable for long-term storage. However, there is enough room for temporary storage of smartphones, glasses, keys, etc. If you mount it on the wall of a Japanese-style room and place a shrine talisman on it, it can become a modern household Shinto altar (*Kamidana*).

You may be worried that the shelves will tilt if you just put hemp string on them, but the string is actually just for decoration. The shelves are stronger than they look because they are firmly screwed to the posts.

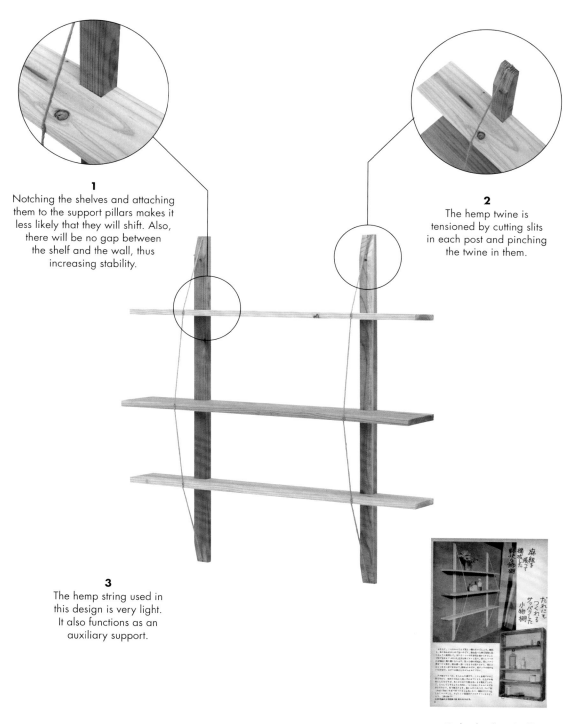

1

Notching the shelves and attaching them to the support pillars makes it less likely that they will shift. Also, there will be no gap between the shelf and the wall, thus increasing stability.

2

The hemp twine is tensioned by cutting slits in each post and pinching the twine in them.

3

The hemp string used in this design is very light. It also functions as an auxiliary support.

Light display shelf constructed with hemp string, from original publication.

PARTS AND MATERIALS

t = thickness
1 t24 x 30 x 800mm: 2 boards
2 t13 x 90 x 700mm: 2 boards
3 t12 x 150 x 700mm: 1 board
The numbered pieces above are referred to in both the drawings and the instructions.

TOOLS

Double-edged saw, chisel, hammer, clamps, ruler and tape measure, carpenter's square, combination square and angle finder, impact driver, screws (45mm), brass nails (25mm), jute twine, hand planes, electric sander, sandpaper, glue

SIZE OF PARTS

Scale = 1/10
Measurements = mm

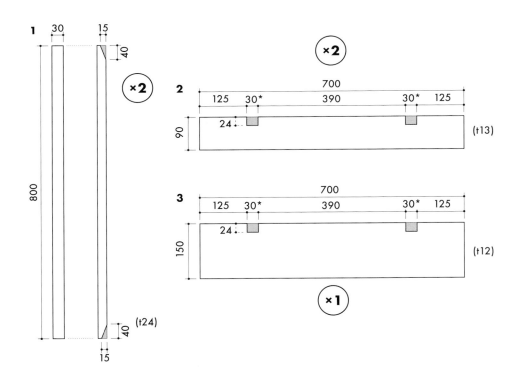

* Measure the actual width of the material to be inserted

DRAWING

Scale = 1/10

Measurements = mm

- ● Screw in from side
- ● Screw in from back
- ○ Brass nail
- ► Screw direction
  (specified as appropriate)

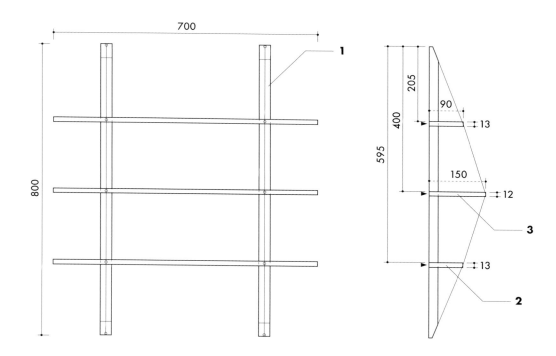

1 Use a ruler, combination square, angle finder and pencil to measure and mark out all the parts.

2 Make cuts for the notches (**2**, **3**). Then make several cuts in the space between the outer cut edges of the notch.

3 Gradually chisel out the notches, moving towards the bottom line. To finish, align the chisel with the bottom line and tap with a hammer to make a clean cut.

4 Cut the tip of the support posts (**1**). Use a rip blade to cut the wood at an angle. The key is to saw slowly and without using much force.

5 Make small slits on the ends of the posts (**1**). Use a saw to cut small V-shaped grooves for the hemp twine to bite into (see inset picture).

6 After processing, sandpaper all parts and chamfer with a hand plane. Corners should be chamfered with sandpaper because they are easily chipped with a hand plane.

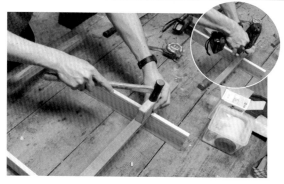

7 Attach the top and bottom shelves to the posts (**1**, **2**). Insert the posts into the shelf notches. Use a small piece of wood to protect the shelves as you gently tap them into place. Once fitted, fasten the screws from the back. (Screws: 45mm)

8 Attach the middle shelf (**3**) in the same way as the previous step. Once the shelf is in place, fasten with screws from the back. (Screws: 45mm)

9 Force the hemp twine into the V-shaped grooves on the posts. Hammer in a brass nail to secure it in place. (Brass nails: 25mm)

10 Lightly apply some tension to the hemp string and secure it to each shelf with brass nails. (Brass nails: 25mm)

11 Secure the other end of the hemp twine by applying firm tension to the end of the twine and forcing it into the V-shaped groove on the other end of the post. Fix with brass nails. (Brass nails: 25mm)

12 When mounting the shelves on the wall, fasten with two screws at the top and bottom of each post.

SLIM DISPLAY SHELVES

This compact display unit is great for showing off your prized collections. Since the depth of the shelf is only 90mm, it is perfect for small cups and accessories, or for organizing children's collectable toys. If you attach a threaded hook under the shelf and place it by the entrance to your home, it can even be used as a key holder. Alternatively, you could make the shelves with different depths.

The wooden frame is reinforced by the plywood backing. It is a simple, but strong, structure. The position and number of the shelves can easily be changed to your liking. The height and depth can also be resized but be sure to install at least one shelf to maintain strength. If you want to mount it on the wall, make holes in the back plate and screw to the wall at the top in at least two points.

1
The parts all have straight lines and right angles, so they can be easily changed to any size you want.

2
The shelves are fastened with screws from the sides. You can change their position to fit your needs.

3
Screws on the back and side panels should be installed at equal intervals for a smoother appearance.

A crisp, clean shelf that anyone can build, from original publication.

PARTS AND MATERIALS

t = thickness
1 t13 x 90 x 660mm: 2 boards
2 t13 x 90 x 374mm: 5 boards
3 t5.5 x 400 x 600mm: 1 board (plywood)
The numbered pieces above are referred to in both the drawings and the instructions.

TOOLS

Ruler and tape measure, carpenter's square, combination square and angle finder, impact driver, screws (35mm, 25mm), hand planes, electric sander, sandpaper, glue

SIZE OF PARTS

Scale = 1/10
Measurements = mm

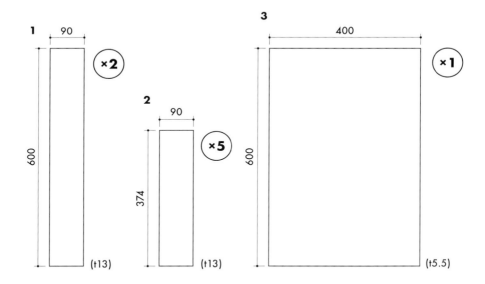

DRAWING

Scale = 1/5

Measurements = mm

- ● Screw in from side
- ● Screw in from back
- ○ Brass nail
- ► Screw direction
  (specified as appropriate)

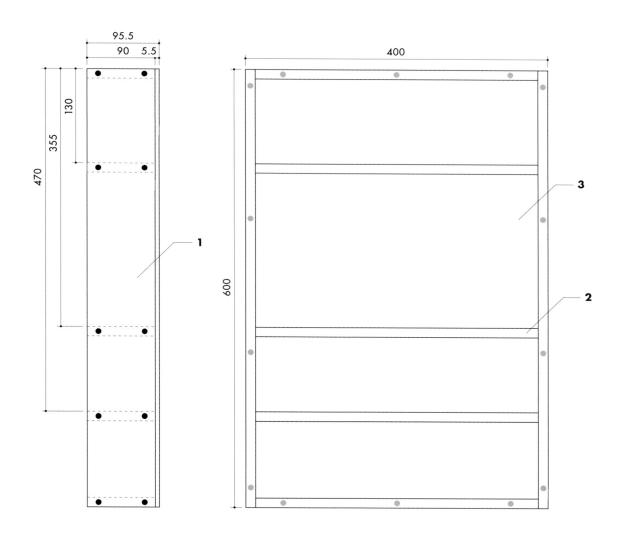

1 Use a ruler, combination square, angle finder and pencil to measure and mark out all the parts.

2 Mark the screw positions onto the side panels. When marking multiple locations at the same interval, use a square piece of wood with the screw locations marked on it as a simple ruler for efficiency.

3 Use a countersink bit to pre-drill the holes. When driving screws into the edge, pre-drilling will prevent splitting. If you use countersunk holes, the screw heads won't protrude and the finish will be much nicer.

4 After processing, sandpaper all parts and chamfer with a plane. The corners should be chamfered with sandpaper because they are easily chipped with a hand plane.

5 Attach the first shelf to one side panel (**1**, **2**). Make sure both parts are flush by placing them on a flat surface and holding them down firmly. Apply glue to the joint and screw together. (Screws: 35mm)

6 Attach the remaining shelves to the side panel. For easy assembly, move your body around instead of the pieces.

7 Attach the second side panel to the other side (**1**, **2**). Start screwing from the outermost shelves. (Screw: 35mm)

8 Lay the frame on a flat surface, rear side down. If any of the corners lift off the surface, move it to the edge of the workbench and straighten by putting weight on the corner.

9 Mark out the screw positions onto the back plate. Prepare a simple ruler using a square stick showing the screw spacing, for easy repetition.

10 Screw on the back plate (**3**). Drill holes at the marked screw positions, then fasten. Use a criss-cross pattern to prevent shifting. (Screws: 25mm)

11 Finish by chamfering the back plate corners. If burrs appear when hand planing, use sandpaper instead.

12 Finish touching up the piece. If there are any areas of concern, use sandpaper to finish them off.

SIMPLE UMBRELLA STAND

04

Time: 3 hours
LEVEL ●●○○○

This slim umbrella stand will fit perfectly along the wall of almost any entrance. The open design allows wet umbrellas to easily dry. The key point is the wavy plate at the top of the unit. If you place your umbrella handle against this plate, it won't fall over, and it will be neatly stored. From a structural point of view, the X-shaped posts are attractive, but it's the upper and lower wooden supports that maintain the strength of the entire structure. When viewed from the side, these parts are designed to form an inverted trapezoid. This is an ingenious way to make the structure less distorted. If the bottom is left unpainted, it may turn black due to mould. If you are concerned about that you may want to paint it with mould-resistant exterior paint.

1

The wavy head piece is important for preventing the umbrellas from falling over. It also serves as a visual accent.

2

The trapezoidal shape of the upper and lower frames is there to prevent them from becoming distorted and to make it easier to insert your umbrellas.

A nifty umbrella stand that is easy to craft, from original publication.

3

The bottom of the stand has a deliberate gap to prevent water droplets from accumulating.

PARTS AND MATERIALS

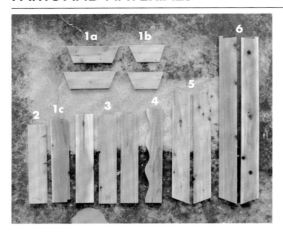

t = thickness
1 t13 x 90 x 424mm: 3 boards
2 t13 x 90 x 398mm: 1 board
3 t13 x 90 x 450mm: 3 boards
4 t13 x 90 x 476mm: 1 board
5 t13 x 90 x 600mm: 2 boards
6 t13 x 90 x 830mm: 2 boards

The numbered pieces above are referred to in both the drawings and the instructions.

TOOLS

Double-edged saw, keyhole saw, clamps, ruler and tape measure, carpenter's square, combination square and angle finder, impact driver, screws (35mm, 25mm), hand planes, electric sander, sandpaper, glue

SIZE OF PARTS

Scale = 1/10
Measurements = mm

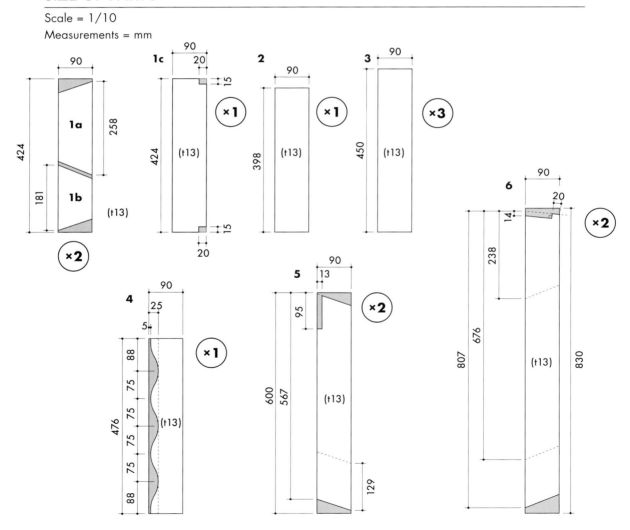

DRAWING

Scale = 1/8

Measurements = mm

- ● Screw in from side
- ● Screw in from back
- ○ Brass nail
- ▶ Screw direction
  (specified as appropriate)

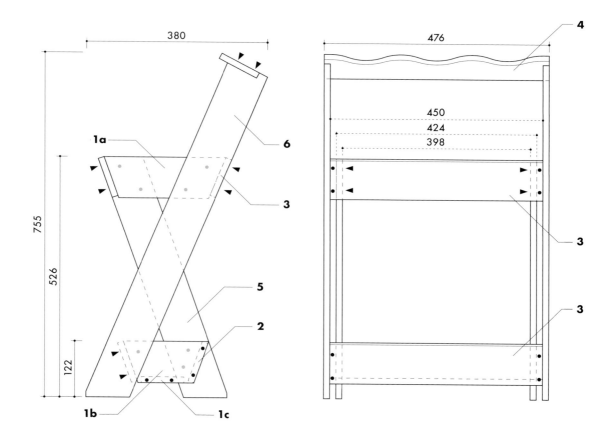

1 Use a ruler, combination square, angle finder and pencil to measure and mark all the parts. Make sure the lines are properly marked. Cut with a saw.

2 Create notches in the support posts (**5**, **6**). Saw first horizontally, then vertically. Cut up to the edge of the marked line, gradually raising the saw until it runs vertical.

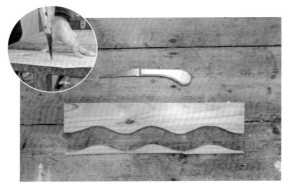

3 Cut the wave shape into piece (**4**) with a keyhole saw. When cutting curved lines, stand the blade up straight and cut downwards.

4 After processing, sandpaper all the parts and chamfer with a plane. The corners should be chamfered with sandpaper because they are easily chipped with a hand plane.

5 Assemble the upper frame (**1a**, **3**). Fasten the screws while making sure there is no overlap along the top edge. Use a countersink bit to pre-drill the holes. Make sure the side panels face the right way. (Screws: 35mm)

6 Assemble the lower frame (**1b**, **3**) in the same way as before, but this time assemble only three sides in a U-shape. Make sure the side panel direction is correct. (Screws: 35mm)

7 Attach the shorter posts (**5**) to the upper frame. Align the support notch with the inside of the frame and screw in place, with the top edge flush. (Screws: 25mm)

8 Pre-drill holes in (**5**) where piece (**2**) will be attached. Use an angle finder to mark the mounting positions and angles. Pre-drill based on the marked lines and fasten. (Screws: 35mm)

9 Attach the lower frame, taking mounting positions from the drawing. Mark them onto the outside of the shorter posts (**5**). Align the lower frame with the marked lines, and screw in place. (Screws: 45mm)

10 Attach the long posts (**6**) to the upper and lower frames. Take measurements from the drawing and mark the mounting positions. Attach posts in line with the marked lines. (Screws: 25mm)

11 Attach the bottom plate (**1c**) to the lower frame. Place it so that the gap is evenly distributed at the front and back. This will prevent rainwater from accumulating. Fasten with screws. (Screws: 35mm)

12 Finish by screwing the wave board (**4**) to the top of the posts. If there is any wobbling, adjust by cutting lower post ends with a saw or by sanding them down.

OPEN-BACK SHOE RACK

This shoe rack is useful for temporarily storing wet leather shoes and muddy sports shoes or boots. It has an open design with no back panel or doors, which allows the air to circulate. In addition, the soles of the shoes are supported by three bars, so even if you put wet shoes on the rack, moisture will not accumulate, and they will dry quickly. Mud and dirt on the soles are collected in a removable tray for easy cleaning.

The side panels are made of 18mm-thick cedar boards. They are thick enough to be sturdy just by attaching the four corners, but what makes this piece even more rigid are the four horizontal boards at the back. This prevents racking. If the side panels were just straight boards, they might look cumbersome, so the leg tips and the upper part are cut diagonally to create lightness.

1

Dirt from the soles of the shoes falls on the plywood. The plywood can be pulled out for easy cleaning.

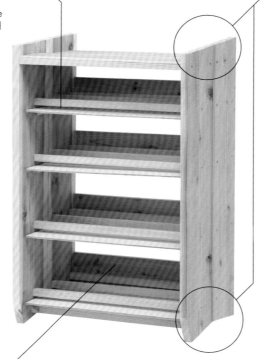

2

Notice the top and bottom of the side panels. The upper part is cut diagonally to make it look more dynamic. The bottom part has an arrowhead shape cut into it to prevent rattling when placed on a dirt floor. This also ensures there is ventilation.

3

The four boards on the back are designed for reinforcement and to maintain air flow.

Easy-to-clean shoe stand, from original publication.

PARTS AND MATERIALS

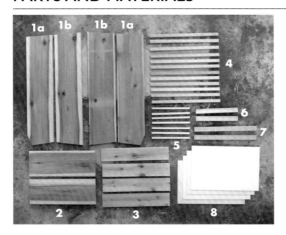

t = thickness
1 t18 x 180 x 800mm: 4 boards
2 t18 x 180 x 450mm: 2 boards
3 t13 x 90 x 450mm: 4 boards
4 t18 x 18 x 450mm: 12 boards
5 t12 x 12 x 260mm: 6 boards
6 t24 x 30 x 275mm: 2 boards
7 t24 x 30 x 402mm: 2 boards
8 t5.5 x 300 x 445mm: 4 boards (plywood)
The numbered pieces above are referred to
in both the drawings and the instructions.

TOOLS

Double-edged saw, clamps, hammer, ruler and
tape measure, carpenter's square, combination
square and angle finder, impact driver, screws
(45mm, 25mm), corrugated nails, hand planes,
electric sander, sandpaper, glue

SIZE OF PARTS

Scale = 1/10
Measurements = mm

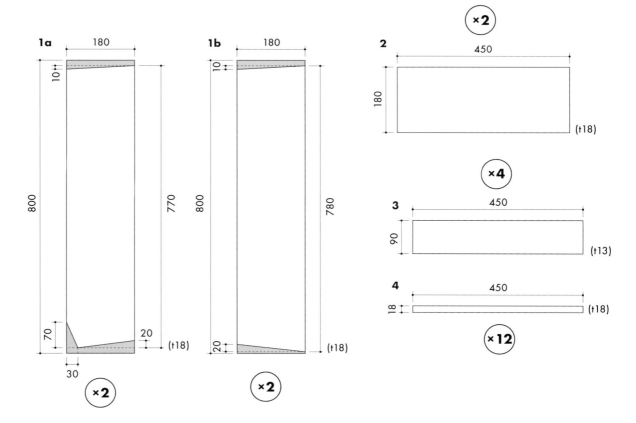

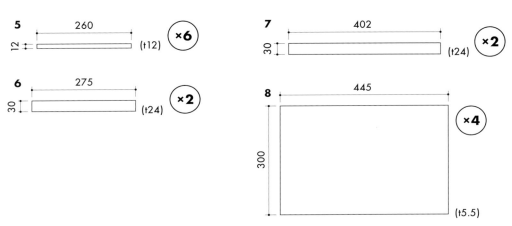

5 260 12 (t12) ×6

6 275 30 (t24) ×2

7 402 30 (t24) ×2

8 445 300 (t5.5) ×4

DRAWING

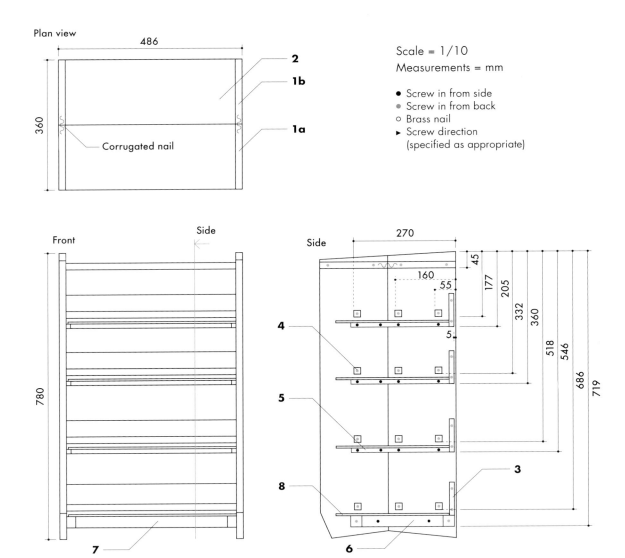

Plan view
486
360
Corrugated nail

2
1b
1a

Scale = 1/10
Measurements = mm

● Screw in from side
● Screw in from back
○ Brass nail
► Screw direction
(specified as appropriate)

Front
Side
780
7

Side
270
45
160
55
177
205
332
360
518
546
686
719
5

4
5
8
6
3

1 Use a carpenter's square and a pencil to mark the material, then saw. Or, you can free saw.

2 Attach cleats (**5**) to the side panels (**1a**, **1b**). Line up the side panels and mark the cleat mounting positions. Use a countersink bit to pre-drill holes in the cleats. Fasten them with screws along the marked lines. (Screws: 25mm)

3 Mark mounting positions for the square supports (**4**) on the inside of the side panels. Pre-drill holes at the screw positions and then use a countersink bit on the exterior side.

4 After processing, sandpaper all the parts and chamfer them with a plane. The corners should be chamfered with sandpaper because they are easily chipped with a hand plane.

5 Assemble the bottom frame parts (**6**, **7**) in a rectangle. Screw them together while pressing down so that the top edge is flush. (Screws: 45mm)

6 Attach the top panel (**2**) and assembled bottom frame to one of the side panels. Fix the two boards of the top together with corrugated nails. Mark the mounting positions. Fasten with screws along the marked lines. (Screws: 45mm)

7 Attach the other side panel. Adjust the top panel and bottom frame as needed and screw in place. (Screws: 45mm)

8 Partially insert screws into all the pre-drilled holes for the square supports (**4**) done in step 3. Doing this means that the screws can be fastened efficiently. (Screws: 45mm)

9 Align the square supports along the marked line. Slowly drive in the screws while pressing down firmly with your hands so that there is no gap between the side panels and square pieces. (Screws: 25mm)

10 Fasten the four backing plates (**3**) with screws, in the same way as step 9. (Screws: 45mm)

11 Screw the opposite side plate on in the same manner. Turn over and repeat steps 8–10. (Screws: 45mm)

12 Finish by sliding the plywood boards (**8**) onto the cleats. Place the rack on a flat surface and check for wobbling. If there is a rattle, adjust by sawing the leg ends or sanding.

Metric to imperial conversion chart

2mm (5⁄64in)	60mm (2³⁄₈in)	210mm (8¼in)	840mm (33in)
3mm (⅛in)	63mm (2½in)	215mm (8½in)	865mm (34in)
4mm (5⁄32in)	65mm (2⅝in)	220mm (8¾in)	890mm (35in)
6mm (¼in)	70mm (2¾in)	230mm (9in)	915mm (36in)
7mm (9⁄32in)	75mm (3in)	235mm (9¼in)	940mm (37in)
8mm (5⁄64in)	80mm (3⅛in)	240mm (9½in)	965mm (38in)
9mm (11⁄32in)	85mm (3¼in)	250mm (9¾in)	990mm (39in)
10mm (⅜in)	90mm (3½in)	255mm (10in)	1015mm (40in)
11mm (7⁄16in)	93mm (3⅔in)	257mm (10⅛in)	1040mm (41in)
12mm (½in)	95mm (3¾in)	280mm (11in)	1065mm (42in)
13mm (½in)	100mm (4in)	305mm (12in)	1090mm (43in)
14mm (9⁄16in)	105mm (4⅛in)	330mm (13in)	1120mm (44in)
15mm (9⁄16in)	110mm (4¼–4³⁄₈in)	355mm (14in)	1145mm (45in)
16mm (⅝in)	115mm (4½in)	380mm (15in)	1170mm (46in)
17mm (11⁄16in)	120mm (4¾in)	405mm (16in)	1195mm (47in)
18mm (23⁄32in)	125mm (5in)	430mm (17in)	1220mm (48in)
19mm (¾in)	130mm (5⅛in)	460mm (18in)	1245mm (49in)
20mm (¾in)	135mm (5¼in)	485mm (19in)	1270mm (50in)
21mm (13⁄16in)	140mm (5½in)	510mm (20in)	1295mm (51in)
22mm (⅞in)	145mm (5¾in)	535mm (21in)	1320mm (52in)
23mm (29⁄32in)	150mm (6in)	560mm (22in)	1345mm (53in)
24mm (15⁄16in)	155mm (6⅛in)	585mm (23in)	1370mm (54in)
25mm (1in)	160mm (6¼in)	610mm (24in)	1395mm (55in)
30mm (1⅛in)	165mm (6½in)	635mm (25in)	1420mm (56in)
32mm (1¼in)	170mm (6¾in)	660mm (26in)	1450mm (57in)
35mm (1⅜in)	178mm (6⅞in)	685mm (27in)	1475mm (58in)
38mm (1½in)	180mm (7in)	710mm (28in)	1500mm (59in)
40mm (1⅝in)	185mm (7¼in)	735mm (29in)	1525mm (60in)
45mm (1¾in)	190mm (7½in)	760mm (30in)	
50mm (2in)	195mm (7¾in)	785mm (31in)	
55mm (2⅛–2¼in)	200mm (8in)	815mm (32in)	

Afterword

I have learned much from the KAK Design Group through the experience of digitally transcribing their drawings, which were created more than 60 years ago, and producing these furniture pieces. I rediscovered how much fun using a saw can be. In most modern DIY projects, power tools are ubiquitous. For those who are used to using power tools, there is an assumption that saws are difficult to cut straight lines with and tire the arm quickly. However, once you can cut smoothly, the sawing process becomes much more interesting. Power tools such as circular saws and jigsaws need to be carefully set up, but a saw can be easily used by supporting the material by hand or securing it with a clamp. After many years, I finally understood the true convenience associated with hand tools.

I also realized that sturdy furniture can be made from soft woods if you keep in mind ways to maintain strength. Points like using V-shaped legs to disperse force and using plywood and wide materials to reduce overall distortion. It was very rewarding to look at the completed works of KAK, as if I was having a dialogue with them through the drawings.

The following words from Yoshio Akioka are strongly engraved in my mind. 'Think carefully about what you want, make it yours. In essence, devise your own tools, use them with all your heart, see how they work, and if you don't like them, think carefully about how to fix them or remake them until you are satisfied... That is the original idea behind manufacturing.'

Yuki Onuma, Furniture Production

First designed and published in Japan © Graphic-sha Publishing Co., Ltd., 2019
Compiled by group monomono
Furniture Production Yuki Onuma (gyutto design)
Designer Katsuharu Takahashi (eats & crafts)
Photographer Takayuki Yoshizaki
Text Supervision Yoshito Kasahara (Kasahara Yoshito Atelier)
Planning Daizen Sugamura (group monomono)
Editor Naoko Yamamoto (Graphic-sha)
Project Manager Takako Motoki (Graphic-sha)
Production Yo Akioka, Meguro Museum of Art, group monomono, AIBA Construction
Company, ReBITA Inc.

Reprinted 2023

The book reproduces wooden furniture extracted from the works of the KAK Design Group
(Yoshio Akioka, Junnosuke Kawa, Itaru Kaneko) in *Aidia wo ikashita katei no kosaku*
(*Making Use of Ingenious Ideas: Woodworking at Home*) (1953, Ondori-sha).
The drawings are recreated from drawings by the KAK Design Group.

Credits for original book: Layout and design: KAK Design Group (as above), Photographs:
Masaya Tobita, Woodworking: Kazunori Yamamoto, Drawing: Yoshiko Akioka, Illustration:
Junnosuke Kawa, Commentary: Itaru Kaneko

This edition coordinated by LibriSource Inc.
Translator Kevin Wilson
ISBN: 978-1-78494-632-6
This English edition was published in 2022 by GMC Publications Ltd.
Publisher Jonathan Bailey
Production Director Jim Bulley
Senior Project Editor Virginia Brehaut
Designers Robin Shields and Ginny Zeal

Picture credits:
Page 11 (bottom right), page 16 (all photos) from KAK albums (the author's private
collection); Page 13 (both), page 15 (top left) and 17 provided courtesy of Meguro
Museum of Art; Page 14 courtesy of Mono Mono; Page 22 (bottom left) and 23 (top) from
Shutterstock.com; Page 23 courtesy of Viva Home Store, Toyosu.

Colour origination by GMC Reprographics
Printed and bound in China

To order a book, contact:

GMC Publications Ltd

Castle Place, 166 High Street,
Lewes, East Sussex, BN7 1XU,
United Kingdom
Tel: +44 (0)1273 488005

www.gmcbooks.com